Journey into Christ

Alan Jones

JOURNEY INTO CHRIST

THE SEABURY PRESS

Typography by Victoria Gomez

Library of Congress Cataloging In Publication Data
Jones, Alan   1940-   Journey into Christ.

Printed in the United States of America

5   4   3   2   1

Winston Press, Inc.
430 Oak Grove
Minneapolis, Minnesota 55403

for Josephine

To see Thee is the End and the Beginning
Thou carriest me and thou goest before
Thou art the Journey and the journey's End.
                        (attributed to King Alfred)

Silence is the attitude in which
we ought to honor the reality of God.
                        (William of St. Thierry)

There is in God (some say)
A deep but dazzling darkness.
                        (Henry Vaughan)

When the inferior man hears about Tao,
he only laughs at it; it would not be Tao
if he did not laugh at it . . . the self-
evidence of Tao is taken for a darkness.
                        (Lao-tse)

Contents

Preface

The material for this book came out of a series of retreat addresses delivered at St. Helena's Convent, Vails Gate, New York. I am indebted to Sister Andrea, O.S.H., for asking me to conduct the long retreat for the Order of St. Helena in 1973. I would also like gratefully to acknowledge a debt to Avery Brooke who made me wait, and to Robert Morris who read the manuscript in its first draft, and helped me to see.

This book would never have come to birth had it not been for the probing encouragement of Madeleine L'Engle, for the persistent enthusiasm of Dr. Dora Chaplin, and for the painstaking textual work of Marcia Greenwood. My wife, Josephine, however, is the one whose quiet support gave the project life. I have tried to keep notes to a minimum and have included a bibliographical note at the end of the book.

September 14th, 1976   *Alan Jones*
Feast of the Exaltation of the Holy Cross   *Little Gidding*
                                                                          Connecticut

1.

The Invitation to Pilgrimage

This is an invitation to go on a journey, a very strange journey. The invitation itself is somewhat out of place since we are already on a journey whether we like it or not. It is our voyage through life into the arms of death, and into the great darkness. For this inevitable journey to become a personal pilgrimage it has to be acknowledged and embraced. The symbolism concerned with this particular voyage is so rich and varied that the ground on which we stand continually shifts. To go on this inner pilgrimage will mean stripping ourselves of our usual expectations when we travel anywhere. There is, for example, no fixed place of departure, no strict timetable, no set itinerary. No mention can yet be made of a destination. The reason is disturbingly simple. This journey is a spiritual one and as such is concerned with the connections we make between inner and outer realities. These realities are often hidden and the would-be voyager should know at the outset of the frustrations and dangers ahead.

The dangers are evident to those who are engaged seriously in psychotherapy or in the direction of souls. The journey inwards (taken lightly) can be the means of unhinging minds, of losing touch with reality, of spiritual aberration and spiritual death. What is meant to be an exploration into a deeper meaning can become instead a frightening encounter with meaninglessness. In a time of great spiritual hunger we are more and more likely to plunge into this journey carelessly in the desperate hope of finding something to eat. In the absence of genuine nourishment the human spirit is forced to feed on any scraps it can find.

The frustrations are also obvious. The word "spiritual" itself presents several problems. To some, the word "spirituality" suggests escapism, inactivity, and irrelevance. To others it suggests full human development in a world where it is hard to be human. "Spirituality" is an unmanageable umbrella word covering a myriad of attitudes and activities from the deeply creative to the distinctively bizarre. It is primarily concerned with our attempt to bind together the crumbled dust of human experience so that life has some semblance of sense. Spirituality, then, is a central term and is used loosely to include *anything* we do in order to structure our universe and stop chaos from breaking in.

We suffer today from the loose use of words such as "charismatic," "mysticism," and "spirituality." They are part of the arsenal of words used by people who fancy that they are religious. As we proceed on our journey the need to rehabilitate language will become manifest.

Spirituality is concerned with the search for wholeness: Christian spirituality with the wholeness that is *given* to us by God in Christ. To talk of a spiritual journey then means to engage in a demanding exercise of great patience. The reason is that the data we have at our disposal is so rich and complex that fixed ways of thinking will not do, particularly in the light of that expanding reality which has been opened up for us by depth psychology, and to which the great mystics have borne perennial witness. We are voyagers toward meaning, toward the double mystery of God and of ourselves, the mystery of Immanuel—God-with-us. We are not, therefore, examining the mechanism of a clock, nor are we exploring the inner workings of a computer. These tasks require skill and knowledge which human beings can acquire in time. Rather we are examining everything, and if we insist on approaching this task in the same way we would a clock or a computer, we are doomed to fail. Aristotle called his study of particulars *Physics* and his study of the way the individual things in the universe hang together *Metaphysics* (thus named because it was written after [*meta*] his *Physics*).

The journey I propose has something to do with how everything hangs together (with metaphysics), how we human beings belong together and make sense as a fellowship. Ours then is a journey of coherence and coinherence: coherence because we are born with this metaphysical urge to make sense of things; coinherence because we make sense *together* in a reality that judges and apprehends us rather than one which we judge and apprehend. Reality, whatever it is, is not held together by our thinking about it but is the given framework for our thinking and doubting, loving and hating. The journey, then, is concerned with discernment, with finding connections, patterns of relatedness, a matrix of conviviality. It is a journey which painfully and slowly seeks to build up meaning for men and women in community as we all move in that unavoidable direction.

On such a journey as this, then, it would be unreasonable for us to expect things to happen in strict chronological order. Nor will we be surprised if the ground continually moves under our feet. We are in a region where silence is the only appropriate response and yet words force themselves upon us out of the silence. How are we to make sense of our experiences as human beings? We live in a world of multiplicity yet it all seems to hang together as a "chaosmos" (to use James Joyce's marvelous word). The philosophers talked of the problem of the one and the many. How can we talk of a *uni*verse when the evidence before our eyes suggests a *multi*verse? This shifts from being a problem to being a mystery for the religious person, and the urgency to explore this mystery becomes insistent. The one and the many, subject and object, individual and community, are problems only insofar as we examine them in isolation. The way through is a spiritual way, a path of stillness and contemplation by which a sense of "everything" is given us. But it is a hard way, for few of us are willing simply to wait.

Read what follows meditatively. Do not suspend your critical faculties, but sharpen them in such a way that the thoughts printed here will prompt you to think on your own. I have tried to avoid mere cleverness with regard to the meaning of ancient or modern myths and ideas. What I hope to do is encourage you to move into that highest of all human activities which we call prayer.

You are invited to go with me on a journey. It is a journey full of danger and risk. It is a voyage into meaning which necessarily involves the menacing possibility of meaninglessness. In the life of the spirit one deep calls to another, and in the chanting of the *De Profundis* we enter the abyss that already exists within us, that "deep but dazzling darkness" in the heart of God himself. The fool laughs at this. Vacuous laughter, however, is poor defense against the demons and dragons of the spiritual life. Indeed the dangers are such that we may have to be touched by what many would reckon as madness.

The journey, then, will require all our energies of mind and heart. It will mean leaving the comfortable familiar world of our day-to-day living. Just as the ancient Israelites were driven by the spirit to leave the fleshpots of Egypt to meet God in the desert, so we will be driven out from where we are now and sent to a place we do not know. We are to be like those early Christians who saw their whole life as a peregrination, a pilgrimage. The journey had its dangers but the pilgrims traveled in hope and in joy because their destination was also their companion. In the words of a prayer attributed to King Alfred: "To see Thee is the end and the beginning. Thou carriest me and Thou goest before. Thou art the journey and the journey's end."

The metaphor of the journey should be neither uncongenial nor unfamiliar to us. This, like every other age, is an age of pilgrimage. We are all on the move. Some of us, however, move aimlessly; or if not aimlessly, at least as though driven by forces beyond our control. We are like those little arctic rodents, the lemmings, who rush into the sea in a suicidal frenzy. There is in all of us a deep fear of, and, paradoxically, a desire for death. Three basic longings haunt us: the desire for triumph over death; the desire for meaning; and the desire for intimacy from which we draw our sense of identity. There are many who specialize in exploiting these desires. In every pilgrimage, as Chaucer knew, there are helpers, hangers-on, experts, inns upon the way: guides, gurus, and procurers of secret knowledge.

For many, Christianity has not only ceased to be *the* way but is no longer even *a* way. At best it is a beautiful idea devoid now of power, absurdly impotent with regard to those twin agonies: the questions of meaning and of death. To many, Christianity no longer seems to be a possible option. We are overcome with nostalgia. While we are repelled by the new fundamentalisms, we long for a direct and simple faith with power to effect our transfiguration. Like the common man in *A Man For All Seasons* we "wish rain water was beer, but it ain't" and our wishing will never make it so.

The twentieth-century voyager might expect to find help and fellowship within the Church. The Church, however, seems too frantically and faithlessly preoccupied with its own interior to have much time for the world it exists to serve. The Church has apparently little or nothing to say to those men and women who are spiritually crippled or impotent. This is an unfair judgment. The Church, as an institution, has always been slow to respond energetically to basic human needs. Nevertheless men and women within the institution have been given the courage to reach out to others with healing and reconciling power.

"Everything that the Lord's teaching absolutely requires of us, Freud claims, is not possible for people who've experienced 'maternal deprivation'," writes a twentieth-century Christian pilgrim in a personal letter. As I read this painful letter in the privileged stillness of my quiet study, it came upon me with unnerving force that the human condition requires a miracle. This book is an attempt to rediscover the miracle of Christianity, its depth and wonder, its transforming power. To those who believe, the Christian way is the power of God even for post-Freudian humanity. For God to be real to my post-Freudian correspondent, or to be real to me, he would need to reveal himself in the experience of forsakenness, numbness, and despair. That would be miraculous indeed. It is no wonder that human beings continue to be fascinated by the figure of the crucified Jesus. Even if we have ceased to believe with any passion, the suffering Christ still speaks to us. Suffering is an inevitable and recurring leitmotif on our journey. The Christian way points to its transformation.

The pilgrim, if he is honest, will have to take the mystery of evil, and more important, will have to encounter the awful possibilities of evil within himself. The journey will involve a kind of crucifixion, an entering into the heart of darkness before the pilgrim can be bathed in light.

We have a clue to the shape of this human adventure in the great works of literature and in the ancient myths and sagas which have been instrumental in molding human consciousness. Underneath the tragedies of human life patterns of meaning, of purpose, of joy can be discerned, but the vision of this benign order is not easily won.

There have been many pilgrims before us who have documented the journey. Homer's *Odyssey,* Dante's *Divine Comedy, The Legend of the Holy Grail,* and more recently Tolkien's *The Lord of the Rings,* can be read as detailed, if fanciful, descriptions of the basic journey of the inner life of every human being.

The phenomenal success of *The Lord of the Rings* cannot be dismissed as escapism or nostalgia. It is a serious exploration of the world of faerie, of myth, of symbolism. It helps to fill the enormous vacuum hollowed out in the soul by secularism and by what has been called the technobarbarism of our age. Depth psychology has done a great deal in mapping out the various stages of this human and, we trust, humanizing journey into the gate of death.

We who are about to die demand a miracle! The miracle we demand and need is nothing less than the double transfiguration of meaninglessness into meaning, of death into life. Intimations that a miracle is possible lie deep within us and prompt us to hazard the voyage. The first intimation of miracle is the gift of life itself, and we are, by virtue of being alive, invited to go on pilgrimage. A human being is a movement, a voyage, and the accumulated evidence of human history suggests that the voyage into our full humanity involves sacrifice and suffering. The miracle for which we long and to which the Christian Gospel bears witness is the promise of joy present at the heart of despair. We have no choice but to move and to risk.

Like Frodo, Tolkien's unprepossessing hero, our beginnings are childlike. We, like him, have to endure the terror of encountering monsters and dragons in the underworld. Yet throughout the marvelous and terrifying adventures of Tolkien's hero (adventures in which we share) there is a steady and profound conviction that everything will turn out for the best. This is not the naïve optimism of a Dr. Pangloss, Voltaire's amusing but pathetic philosopher in *Candide.* It is faith in the possibility of the new, the miraculous, the transfiguring breaking in on human affairs. In other words, Tolkien's story is basically a strong affirmation of faith in the human enterprise. The fundamental affirmation rings true because it is not sentimental. It is a hard won act of faith, refined in the fires of high adventure, purified by the hard lessons of self-giving.

We live in a world where death and tragedy are the commonplace events of human life. There is no way we can avoid them and no way we can feel entirely at home on this planet. Yet death and tragedy are not the only truths we have to face. Underneath these, as Tolkien insists, there abides meaning, purpose, design: miracle. There is joy. There is the deep but dazzling darkness of love. The miracle of Christianity is precisely this, that in the face of tragedy, exile, and the final bankruptcy of death, there is hope of new life. There is wholeness. There is resurrection. In the end it is a matter of faith, a matter of love. No one can argue himself into belief in the miracle of resurrection, of new life.

This then is no sentimental journey. It involves a death, but also a glimpse of joy, a sharing in new life, and a new beginning for the world.

2.

Preparation for Pilgrimage

LOSS OF MYTH AND SYMBOL

> Towards the end of seven days the waters of the flood came
> upon the earth. In the year when Noah was six hundred
> years old, on the seventeenth day of the second month, on
> that very day, all the springs of the great abyss broke
> through, the windows of the sky were opened, and rain fell
> on the earth for forty days and forty nights.
>
> *Genesis 7:10–12*

Storm and flood begin our journey. There are no promises, no guarantees, not even an itinerary. We travel lightly, just as we are. The sky is overcast. There is a heavy promise of tempest, fire, and flood. The ship on which we are to take the first part of our journey is about to weigh anchor. We must hurry.

The story of Noah's ark is significant for would-be voyagers. The floodwaters are present as Noah pioneers a new beginning for the world. Water has a double significance here: new birth—in the same way that the waters had to be broken over us at our physical birth—and the possibility of destruction and chaos as we begin the new life. The possibility of meaning and the threat of meaninglessness come to us simultaneously in the flood. Tempest is its inevitable concomitant. So there is danger which requires courage and faith. Our three desires come to the fore again: for meaning, for triumph over death; the third, the desire for intimacy, for community, is met in the fact that the coming flood requires Noah to build an ark, in which the community is preserved. We will be saved or we will drown *together*.

New birth, with its attendant dangers and new courage, brings with it new community of which the ark is a potent symbol—storm-tossed but intact on the floodwaters. The ark of Noah is an ancient image of the Church, the one sure haven in a chaotic world. But the ark had no rudder. There was no means by which Noah could guide his ship. Rudderless and lost, he flung himself into that mystery which we call God. The journey of the rudderless boat tossed to and fro by the wind of God is a common theme in literature. Noah was not the only one who abandoned himself to the providence of God. There were many others, who, in the imagery of abandonment, lostness, darkness, faith, and trust, were tempest-tossed in their flimsy boats. They risked all for the joy that was set before them. We, the Church, the human race, also live in a time of great flood. All of us experience it. We are all fellow passengers on the ark and no matter how uncongenial we are to one another, we can never be complete strangers during this cruise.

The romantic version of this voyage is found in the Arthurian Cycle, particularly those sections which deal with the quest for the Holy Grail. An important, if subsidiary, part of the Arthurian Cycle deals with the story of Tristan and Iseult. On the surface it is one of many romantic stories about star-crossed lovers. There are many versions of this story and many interpretations. This is a version which illustrates the theme of the rudderless boat. Tristan, a minstrel, is the nephew of Mark, the King of Cornwall. His adventures take him to Ireland, where a deep wound is healed by Iseult, the beautiful daughter of an Irish king. On his return to Cornwall, Tristan tells his uncle of the fair princess, and King Mark resolves to wed her himself. He sends Tristan as his ambassador to bring his bride home. On the way back to England a magic potion binds Tristan and Iseult to one another forever in love. Tristan has to flee to Britanny where he marries another Iseult (to add more confusion to an already confused story). In Brittany Tristan sustains another wound from a poisoned weapon and he sends for Iseult of Ireland to heal him. The ship is to bear a white sail if she is on board, a black if not. His jealous wife lies and tells Tristan the ship coming into harbor bears a black sail. In despair Tristan dies, and his true love kills herself.

The story is conventional enough and has many parallels: Heloise and Abelard, Romeo and Juliet. We need to cut through the romance to get to the heart of the story. Tristan represents us all. He carries within him both a wound and a gift: the wound of love and the gift of love. Like Tristan, each one of us carries a treasure waiting to be shared. The wound is deep and is the result of our triple tragedy: the threat of meaninglessness, the inevitability of death, and the loss of intimacy. The treasure is the seed of hope which promises the transfiguration of the wound into the source of healing itself, bringing meaning, the promise of a lost integrity, and the final triumph over death.

The treasure we seek is not hard to find. Our heart's desire is already present within us. One of the great stories in the Hasidic tradition speaks of this treasure that lies deep within us. Isaac, a poor Jew, lived in a grim hovel many miles from a great city. One night he dreamed that if he were to make the long trek to the far-off city, he would find a bag of gold hidden under the bridge leading to the main gate. Isaac was so poor that he had nothing to lose in hazarding everything on what, at first sight, seemed such a fool-hardy venture. So he made his way painfully and slowly to the city. He arrived footsore and weary after many days of walking. To his dismay the bridge leading to the main gate was heavily guarded. Forlorn and lost, Isaac loitered there under the bridge hoping for an opportunity to make a search for the treasure. His agitated presence soon caught the eye of the captain of the guard. "What are you doing here, old man?" he shouted down to Isaac. Isaac, in the simplicity of his poverty, told his dream to the captain. Scarcely able to contain his laughter, the captain replied, "Why, you old fool, where would we be if we took notice of our dreams? Why, only last night, I dreamed that if I were to journey to a small village miles from here, I would find some treasure hidden behind the fireplace in the miserable hovel of an old Jew named Isaac! Be off with you, old man. This is foolishness!" Isaac made his way home as fast as he could. And, of course, he found the treasure behind his own hearth. The meaning of this story is not difficult to see. The treasure which we seek is very close to us, under the hearth, in our hearts. But in order to discover this inner treasure, we must go on a long journey. Unless we go on pilgrimage, we will never be able to return home.

As the story of Isaac points to the treasure in every human heart, so the story of Tristan and Iseult bears witness to the wound which we all carry. Once we begin to penetrate the stories, myths, and legends which weave themselves around human destiny, we see that even such disparate ones as that of Isaac the Jew and Tristan and Iseult throw light on our inner secrets. The theme of the wound finds echoes in all our hurts, in all our disappointments, in all our failures. We long for a cure, for a miracle. That is why Noah built the ark.

So the minstrel Tristan, stinking and rotting from his wounds, sails to Ireland in his little coracle to his cure. He lies languishing from a deep sword-cut but, strangely, is unable to die of it. He had been attacked by pirates and put in a rudderless boat in which he drifted for forty days and forty nights. It is not hard to guess what was in the writer's mind here. As the children of Israel sojourned in the wilderness for forty years before they entered the promised land, as Jesus fasted for forty days and forty nights, so Tristan suffered and waited in his fragile craft. His journey is a prerequisite for his cure. The deep, the desert, the wilderness: all represent abandonment, alienation, lostness. All are integral to our journey. All are preparatory disciplines for the genuine treasure-seeker.

"We are all in the same boat" takes on new significance. Our boat, too, happens to be rudderless: the Ark of Noah, the Coracle of Tristan, the Bark of Peter—and the Ship of Fools. This basic human condition which poets write about, with which philosophers struggle, has various names: original sin, the fall, or, nowadays, the environment. It is the working out of the free drama of our lives in the given theater of this world.

Why all this talk of abandonment and extremity, of tempest and wounding? Why all this preparation for a journey? To rescue us from the easy answers and shallow security offered us by "moralism." Moralism is the doctrine that man is perfectible by his own efforts. There are basically two forms: rigorist and permissive. Both reduce us to the terms of this world, and both fail to see us as pilgrims.

The rigorist does it by planning the route of the human journey in detail from the safe haven of rule and precedent. He places himself beyond the reach of danger and confrontation by weaving patterns of protective legislation which reduce the possibility of risk and obliterate forever the hope of adventure.

The libertine, on the other hand, imagines that he has found true freedom in the impenetrable darkness of his own chaos. The rigorist wants to enforce a morality on others; the libertine wishes to dispense with morality altogether. The true adventurer, however, strives to transcend morality and discover the heady freedom that exists on the other side of convention.

The image of the rudderless boat bears witness to a givenness, to a condition in which recreative grace alone can operate and save. A boat without a rudder cannot guide itself. The voyagers are forced to accept the guidance of the wind which blows where it will. Only something or someone beyond the boat can bring it to a safe haven. We who are about to die demand a miracle! We have to stop trying to save ourselves. We even have to stop striving not to strive before anything creative and loving can happen to us, before the real journey can begin.

The Christian claims that the journey is a voyage to love in the company of love; and the life of love presupposes communion with the loved one. But this affirmation does not remove the danger or the risk involved. We are still in the fragile coracle sailing apparently aimlessly on the formless sea of what, in faith, we believe to be the love and providence of God. We have no choice but to wait. Silence, contemplation, prayer—these are the means by which the voyager ventures into the heart of things. The waiting which prayer involves is sometimes unbearable. This is why the thought of praying fills me, on occasion, with an undisguised dread, even disgust. Prayer invites me to stand still when all I want to do is run. There are enormous dangers to be found in the deeper recesses of the soul. There was a time when I could enjoy a brief excursion into prayer, a day or two of monkish observances to brush away the cobwebs of the world. These stabs at holiness seemed harmless enough then, but will scarcely suffice now. The vision of what is and what might be fills me with "a deep but dazzling darkness." Prayer, not to say contemplation, and the absurdity of *telling* people about that voyage called meditation, is now, for me, a hazardous, often bizarre, always challenging, enterprise. It is exposure; it is a deliberate opening of the heart and mind for rebirth. It is the price one pays for commitment to the conviction that human beings and reality, truth, integrity, meaning, are all fellow passengers in the ark.

The journey involves the exploration of images, mythologies, ideas, pictures in the hope that one or two may become an icon, a window into reality, a compass by which we may cross uncharted waters. The ark of Noah had no rudder but this does not mean that it was left unguided. Two principles guided the ark: the faith of Noah and the faithfulness of God. It was this strange conjunction which brought the vessel to safety. Our journey also requires such faith and faithfulness. Faith and faithfulness help us to receive the miracle when it comes. But faith in what? On whose faithfulness does the journey depend? Our faith and God's faithfulness come together in Christ, the great voyager through the gate of death. The faith which guided Noah, Abraham, and Moses was prompted by the call of God: to Noah to build the ark, to Abraham to leave his homeland, to Moses to lead his people out of Egypt.

Christ is the focus of all these aspirations: the alpha and the omega, the first and the last. He confronts us in startling particularity, calling us to follow him. He is "the journey and the journey's end." But we have mummified him, made of him a plastic replica. Instead of embarking on a pilgrimage we stay where we are, worshiping an idol manufactured and refined within the workshop of our own psyche. We bow down before the totem of our own prejudices and projections. Our emaciated Christianity will not do, cut off as it is from any genuine source of power, but neither will "a pallid humanitarianism." Both lead nowhere. If Christ is not the faithful one, is not God himself, then there is no point bothering with this long-dead rabbi. It is better to try the journey alone. Unless Christ is the one in whom our faith and the faithfulness of God meet there can be no homecoming.

Ours is a journey home (wherever that is) which involves a giant step into the unknown. It asks us to allow ourselves to be stripped of everything so that we can begin to make this pilgrimage unhampered across uncharted waters.

The great voyagers (Noah, Abraham, Moses) found out who they were in the giant step of faith. In the pilgrimage they not only discovered the secret of their identity but also understood that their identity was held together not so much by their faith as by God's faithfulness. In the great ocean of the faithfulness of God we are cut off from our moorings and driven out into the deep. The wind blows us away from our comfortable and well-established patterns of thinking, whether they be traditional ones or those forged out of current sociological or psychological orthodoxies.

What makes the spiritual journey both exciting and terrifying is its hiddenness. The God that we worship is hidden from us. He is beyond any possibility of our manipulation or control. He is free. Yet we are made "after his image and likeness." If he is the God who hides himself and we are made in his image, then we too are hidden from ourselves: "it doth not yet appear what we shall be" (1 John 3:2). The psalmist understood something of this: "But as for me, I will behold thy presence in righteousness: and when I awake up after thy likeness, shall be satisfied with it" (Psalm 17:15).

Let us attempt, then, a journey of self-discovery by venturing into the darkness and hiddenness of God. It is in him that we shall "know even as we are known." The hiddenness of God is that which safeguards human freedom. Human beings tend to tyrannize and even brutalize others with the god they have uncovered for themselves. The hidden God, however, cannot be used, nor can he be pinned down by definitions or expectations—and neither can we.

We cannot delay. Time does not stop. The journey has already begun. Its hidden, secret quality drives us into a world of strange reversals and frustrating opposites, of sitting still yet always moving, of praying and not praying, of waiting on God but ever searching for him, of letting the self go and allowing the self to be. It is in this "conjunction of opposites," of striving not to strive, that we will begin the journey into the freedom of God. We will begin to encounter the mystery of who we are, the mystery of the living God who made "the sun and all the stars."

This first step into the hiddenness of God is a hard one: it is a deliberate act of *un*learning. We think we know who we are; we have some idea of what it is to be a human being, even to be a Christian. These ideas for the most part, have to be abandoned.

Unlearning is particularly hard for us. We have been conditioned into thinking that our learning, our expertise, is the one thing that keeps us on top, that helps us to keep up with the leaders of the pack. To unlearn something would threaten our position, our status, our identity. Unlearning is as risky as Noah's climbing into the ark. It is closely linked with the image of the tiny, fragile coracle of Tristan. Both bear witness to the vulnerability and insecurity involved in the voyage. It would not be in our best interest to unlearn things; nor is it reasonable to commit ourselves to flimsy boats. Given our pitifully limited vision, it would be absurd to endure the ignominy of unlearning with no guarantee of a final triumph or justification.

As our vision of things deepens and expands, we are forced to unlearn things whether we like it or not. New insights demand that we abandon or adjust acquired skills. In the realm of the spirit we have to become a child if we are to see the world once again with any wonder. Becoming a little child is no easy thing. There is a toughness to the process which can be terrifying. What could be more humiliating to twentieth-century, "successful" Western adults than to embrace once again the helplessness and the playfulness of a child? Unless we do just that, we will never experience the deep joy that only awe can give, nor will we catch a glimpse of the love which beats in the heart of everything. To become a child is to see the world and be overcome by its brilliance and dazzled by its wonder.

The adult's joints are stiff. The child's limbs are supple. Habit, laziness, and cynicism make it hard for the so-called grown-up to move and to unlearn the bad habits of a lifetime. It is the child who can help us unlearn those dogmas (regarding failure and success in the world's terms) which enslave us. It is the child who adds the vital ingredient of hilarity, humor, and play to what would be an overly intense and gruesome journey.

Becoming a child in adult life is peculiarly difficult because there is always the tendency to lapse into childishness. The risk has to be taken for the sake of joy and laughter. Without the childlike dimension the journey becomes self-consciously grim, and the voyager becomes taken up by his own dread seriousness of purpose. The child and the joker are necessary, humiliating, and deflating companions. Humor punctures our pretensions. Romantic voyagers tend to take themselves too seriously. There is a story (invented by Max Beerbohm) of the great Dr. Benjamin Jowett encountering Dante Gabriel Rosetti in Oxford. Rosetti was busy painting the themes of ancient chivalry, and in particular the legend of the quest for the Holy Grail. It was all very romantic, all very pretentious. Jowett asked him the joker's unforgiveable question: "And what were they going to do with the Grail when they found it, Mr. Rossetti?" No question could be more deflating nor more necessary for the questing soul. As we go deeper it would be well to keep this story in mind. The dangers of the quest are enormous enough, but perhaps the greatest peril lies in our taking ourselves desperately seriously. The deeper we go the more we will be tempted to romanticize the journey, and become self-consciously intense.

Unlearning and hiddenness for the adult means entering the wasteland, waiting, waiting, *Waiting for Godot.* The wasteland theme in literature presents us with a landscape of spiritual death, a sense of being cut off. We are deliberately unlearning, exposing ourselves to the elements. To be sure, the wasteland is not all there is. Eliot knew that, as did Dante; but poets, artists, and saints know that the journey through the desert, or, to use Dante's image, through the dark wood, has to be made before we can truly enter creatively into those twin mysteries of meaning and death.

Much of the trouble we pass through is, naturally, of our own making. The monsters we encounter have been put together by our follies and machinations. The wasteland (one image of the spiritual world after two world wars) is largely our invention. There is, however, an intransigence, a stubborness about things which is *given* us. We did not conjure up all the troubles and monsters which lie in our path. This recalcitrant and menacing givenness is symbolized by the desert. The wasteland and the desert, therefore, are not identical. We make the wasteland for ourselves; the desert is given to us. These two images point to the fact that our condition is both given and manufactured.

Many of us still think we know where we are and what is happening to us. George Orwell, writing during the Second World War, tells of

a rather cruel trick I once played on a wasp. He was sucking jam on my plate and I cut him in half. He paid no attention, merely went on with his meal, while a tiny stream of jam trickled out of his severed oesophagus. Only when he tried to fly away did he grasp the dreadful thing that had happened to him. It is the same with modern man. The thing that has been cut away is his soul and there was a period—twenty years perhaps—during which he did not notice it. It was absolutely necessary that the soul be cut away. Religious belief, in the form that we had known it, had to be abandoned.[1]

Our first temptation in this wasteland, cut off from our soul, our selves, is to construct a shelter as quickly as possible from the debris of our shattered aspirations. Perhaps therapy will help, or a course in Zen, or a program of renewal (what, again!) or even a trip (metaphorically or literally) into the Orient, or into the new turned-on, charismatic Jesus-world. Do not misunderstand me. Not one of these things is bad in itself, but it may be the very thing with which we—in our panic to leave proportion, humor, and childlikeness behind—desperately try to cover our nakedness. We become a follower of causes, of fads. We can make an idol of anything (that is our genius), even of the poor and underprivileged. It is very easy to posture, to pose for God, and to see ourselves bathed in an artificial light. Therapy at its best, Zen Buddhism at its deepest, Christianity at its heart—do not remotely represent attempts to trivialize and manipulate the mystery.

We are forever seeking to attain a secure if cheap equilibrium. We search for the golden mean between desolation and joy. The stoic within us longs for the numbing consolation of a properly balanced existence. It never works out that way. If only the world would stand still, just for a moment, so that we could take our bearings. Just as we think we have found a firm footing we are knocked violently, sometimes brutally, off our feet. We are forced to abandon our secure haven and be on the move. Reality bears in upon us, and when that happens, we find ourselves at a crossroads, at a crisis point, a moment of decision. When we have been struck down, forced to abandon our safe tower, two ways lie open before us: the way of resentment and the way of joy. It is as if, at the crucial moment when anger rises up in us, we carry a bowl in our two hands. The bowl is a significant image from Tibetan Buddhism. It contains all our bitterness, disappointment, hardness, and disillusionment. There we are holding it in front of us. We can either pour the contents of the bowl forward and allow the whole resentful mess to flow away from us, or we can tip it the other way, pour it into ourselves, and allow the poison to infect our blood. For the one who, in that split second, is given the grace to pour the bowl of bitterness onto the receiving earth and not into himself, there is the beginning of the recognition of the creative love in the deep but dazzling darkness of God. He begins to see God at work summoning him to a joy which makes all the happiness he has hitherto enjoyed as nothing.

On this voyage (which we have already begun whether we want to or not) each one of us is at a crisis point and a decision of sorts has to be made: too much self-concern, too much scratching at the navel, can be damaging. A too careful love of life can be a sign of death. The greatest strength of our life is the power to resign it. This hidden strength rots away while we insist on hugging it in our arms. Some of us are numb, some of us apprehensive, some of us frankly indifferent, some of us expectant. We are going to wait together in the wasteland, wait as quietly and still as we can. Wait. As our eyes get used to the strange light, shapes will begin to appear, familiar yet unfamiliar. It is then we can begin to move, to explore.

"It is a full great pleasure," says Julian of Norwich, "to our courteous Lord that a helpless soul comes to him simply, plainly, homely." We are to come as we are. We may have a cold feeling, like a clod of earth in a frozen field. All right! Even now something is going on in us, even now we are being *made*. Still, here in the wasteland we can begin to learn that there is glory in our feeling of desolation and incompleteness.

This land is full of weird objects and strange beings. You may even meet a *you* you never knew existed.

3.

Entering the Wasteland

THE PLACE OF DARKNESS

The ark and the wasteland are two images which point to danger and adventure. Both are pregnant with hope and despair. The coracle is an image of aimlessness; the wasteland one of desolation. Yet in this directionless, formless environment are present great possibilities. The process of unlearning terrifies us, and in our fear we cry for help and seek old securities. But we may learn to sing a new song in a strange land. In time the wasteland loses its menacing power. This, we realize, is not all there is. It is but one stage on a long journey, at the end of which there is singing and laughter.

The child and the joker accompany us on our journey. They are actors in the drama which tells a tale of loss and terror, of times of initiation and rebirth, of the promise of laughter in a fuller life. But first we must enter the wasteland, a land well traveled by pilgrims through the ages. In this century it was superbly mapped and documented by T. S. Eliot. The wasteland is characterized both by a deep sense of disappointment and hopelessness, as well as a conviction that the sense has gone out of things. The terrain is both bleak and alien. As our eyes get used to the darkness we will begin to see.

Look! Rocks, stones, mountains are given shape in the twilight. It is time to explore the wasteland, which is rooted in the world of poetry, of memory, of mythology. It is through these that we will be able to enter into the mystery.

The formlessness, the emptiness, the void—these are unavoidable and are the various words used to denote that which lies at the heart of human consciousness. The great mystics have struggled to describe it. Depth psychology has helped us to enter it creatively. It is the place of the spirit, the arena in which the self emerges. The infinite emptiness of the human heart is first experienced as terror. When we are content to wait, it is transformed into an eager emptiness waiting to be filled.

Paradoxically, this formlessness needs an outer structure in which to rest if it is to be used creatively. Mere formlessness points to a destructive nihilism. The mystery is, as it were, a jewel that needs a setting. It requires a web of finely spun thread to keep it in place. The human race has traditionally spun stories, sagas, and myths to focus the mystery, to give shape to the emptiness. A rigid dogmatism destroys the mystery, a beautifully woven story provides both a structure and a point of entry.

Problems arise because human beings are creatures of language. We must speak even of those mysteries which evoke a silent response. We struggle with words in order to do justice to the mystery and safeguard its hiddenness and immensity. Religious language is a sort of device which continually frustrates our attempt to bring the mystery down and trim it to fit our parochial point of view. Yet the web of finely spun thread which guards the mystery can easily become the trap which ensnares us. We tend to make the fatal error of mistaking the web for the mystery. We fall down and worship an idol. We cannot distinguish between our images of reality and reality itself.

The incomprehensibility of God is not that of a philosophical concept. In the end, God's hiddenness is in the incomprehensibility of love. Lovers understand this. We know that genuine love depends on a free disclosure of one person to another. The loved one is inaccessible, hidden, free. To *demand* that the lover reveal himself would be to destroy the very ground of loving. Love and freedom require, then, a hiddenness. Love is an abyss. When it is uncovered it comes to us always as a free gift. Around the mystery we weave our patterns, spin our webs and tell our stories.

We must abandon, therefore, the naïve definition of a myth as simply a story which is not true. The coming together of anthropology, depth psychology, and comparative religion has made it clear that a myth, far from being an untruth, is an expression of a deep truth which can be expressed only in poetic or story form. The myth of Adam and Eve is true. We run into difficulty only if we insist on seeing truth as flat and one dimensional. Literalism and truth are not synonymous. The world of mythology opens us up for deeper truths untouched by our technological expertise and narrowly conceived science.

Time ran a story with the headline, "Is The Bible True?" There is only one way in which a magazine can deal with or manipulate truth; that is, as flat and one-dimensional. The biblical story or myth is rooted in history, but what is startling is what it says *about* history, and not only history in general but *my* history and *your* history. Is the Bible true? Is *Hamlet* true? Is Picasso's *Guernica* true? The answer to each question is "Yes"! But there is no way of proving it, at least not to *Time*'s satisfaction. Beyond these questions are deeper ones: Am I true? Do I mean anything? Truth and meaning for individuals and for communities are wrapped up in story form. That is why images and myths are so important.

Joseph Campbell in his work, *The Masks of God,*[2] claims that all mythologies, both ancient and modern, have a fourfold function. The first is somehow to reconcile and relate the waking consciousness to the *mysterium tremendum et fascinans,* to the mystery of being. Awe and wonder are necessary prerequisites for "dwelling in reality" in any total sense. Awe and wonder are required if the whole story is to be told, if meaning and truth are to meet and inhabit us. The basic metaphysical question which has to be posed but to which there is no answer—indeed can be no answer—is: "Why is there anything at all and not just nothing?" Or as the philosopher Wittgenstein put it: "It is not how things are in the world that is mystical, but that it exists."

The second function of mythology is to provide an interpretive framework for the universe; that is, to offer a coherent cosmology and to place man firmly, and if possible safely, within it. The third function is to provide at least the skeleton of social organization; a system of sentiments uniting people. The fourth and most important function of mythology is to initiate us into the inner realities of the soul; to foster our inner growth, to create an environment in which we can *be* in the fullest sense. Our life, to make any joyful sense, must be a system of interconnections by which we are kept in touch with ourselves, with our society and culture, with the universe, and with that awesome ultimate mystery which is both beyond and within us and in all things, and which we call God.

Not all myths and stories, however, are of equal value. Some are downright demonic in that, far from weaving a web around the mystery to hold it in place, they choke it to death and devour it with frightening intensity. As we have seen, the web ceases to guard the mystery. It becomes its destroyer. Myth-makers and storytellers are dangerous in that they mesmerize men and women and force them to live the story they have invented. The individual is lost and as good as dead when he has no story of his own to live. The Reverend Sun Moon is as powerful a myth-maker as are the dedicated evangelists of any religion. Which story is "right"? Do we have any criteria for judging the great stories of our age? A story has to be lived and, in the end, it is a matter of faith which story we choose. Nevertheless, we can distinguish between those stories that build up patterns of creative relatedness and those that do not. We can ask ourselves: How does each story respond to the three-fold need for meaning, for intimacy, and for triumph over death? We will be wary of those stories that offer easy solutions and sentimental happy endings. The hunger for relatedness, for intimacy, for conviviality is linked in the great stories of the world with the inevitability of loneliness, of emptiness, of the hiddenness of God. Genuine intimacy is given only to those who have learned to live creatively within their own solitude. A true story must give an account of all the facts—including death and dissolution.

The Christian myth is awesomely realistic and concrete; its roots are in actual history, in events that really happened. "God so loved the world that he gave his only begotten Son" (J 3:16), is a given, a fact of the universe. It was an act in which reality was reconstituted. It was a new creation. Christ's death and resurrection are both particular events in history and yet events which have changed history; more important, they have revolutionized human possibilities by enabling men and women to share in the divine, to enjoy the being of God. So Christianity's claims are total and far-reaching. They are not the net in which Christians have finally trapped God in majesty. Christians see the whole universe caught up in the incomprehensibility of the love of God.

For many, however, the Christian story no longer bears the mystery. It seems to trivialize it. The Christian way of looking at, interpreting, understanding the world has lost its power. It has become sterile, dead, lost behind a mountain of custom, habit, and convention. We have the outlines of the story, but there are precious few living characters in its half-forgotten and emaciated plot.

Jews in Eastern Europe in the eighteenth century were particularly hard pressed, and when times were extraordinarily harsh the Baal Shem Tov would take himself off to a particular part of the forest to meditate and pray. He would first light a fire, then recite a special prayer. After this, the danger or misfortune facing the little struggling Jewish community would be averted. There would be a miracle.

The Baal Shem's disciple, the Maggid of Mezeritch tried to maintain this tradition after the master's death. When disaster struck the community, he, too, would go into the forest, find the spot where the master had prayed. He was not, however, completely familiar with the ritual practiced by the Baal Shem. All he could say was, "Lord of the Universe, hear me! I know nothing about lighting the fire. All I can do is say the prayer." It was enough. The disaster was averted. The little community could live in peace.

Later on it fell to Moseh-Leib of Sassov to bear the responsibility for the people. When tragedy threatened, he, too, would go into the forest and simply say, "Alas, I do not know the prayer. At least I know the place. This is the best I can do." Again the miracle happened and the people were saved.

Finally, the burden fell on the shoulders of Israel of Rizhin. When misfortune struck all he could do was to sit in his chair with his head in his hands. He addressed God in this way: "O Lord, I cannot light the fire and I have no idea about the prayer. Even the place is hidden from me. The best I can do is to tell the story. This will have to do." The mere telling of the story was enough to avert misfortune.

Those who read aloud to small children know the power of storytelling. Stories have to be repeated, and repeated exactly. The repetition of the familiar story guarantees the integrity and reliability of the universe. Oft-repeated stories have a great power regardless of content. Is there a myth, a story, that reflects all we know about human life? What story can do justice to the terror and the glory of human life? Is there a story in which joy and suffering, happiness and pain, laughter and death, come together? Is there a story, the proclamation of which releases healing power? Christianity claims to be this story, the story by which all other stories are judged. Christians have lost a sense of the saving power of their story. We voyagers without maps need to unlearn and relearn the Christian story. It may yet again be for us, as it has been for millions before us, the bearer of life, the way.

Unlearning and relearning is part of the necessary healing process by which the mystery is released from its ensnaring web. Without it we are like Orwell's severed wasp, sucking away and blissfully unaware of the dreadful thing that has happened to us; unaware, that is, until we once more try to take to the air. We will never be able to fly until we learn again the place in the forest, the gift of fire, and the need for prayer. We have to give up the arrogance of mere technocratic knowledge and begin to relate once again the Christian story in the hope that telling it will be enough to bring about the miracle.

We must ask ourselves the four great questions. Does the Christian story help us to understand and interpret the cosmos? Does the telling of it inform and shape our understanding of social structures and human relations? Does it provide a focus for our own unfolding? With the fading of the Christian story we have been forced to fill in the gaps with other mythologies. There are other stories that have had and still have "miraculous" power in our time.

Let us look for a moment at some of these other modern mythologies, these stories we tell our children. We have witnessed five great mythologies at work during this century. There has been the English myth, which has all but withered and died; the American myth, which is tarnished and frayed; the Nazi myth, now hopefully defunct; and the twin myths of Russian and Chinese Marxism (by no means identical) which are now told with such passionate intensity.

The English myth came into its own in the nineteenth century under Queen Victoria. It was a magnificent story, one which I had been told for as long as I can remember. English law and custom had spread to the far corners of the earth. The continents of Africa and Asia, as well as North America and Australia, had been blessed by the British presence, the *Pax Britannica.* There was even some truth—perhaps a great deal—in this picture. For believing Englishmen it was obvious that God had had a hand in the spread of the empire, of influence, and of the Gospel. The web was spun around the mysterious process of history and many minds made the fatal mistake of confusing the delicate web for the reality itself. The mystery of God was reduced to serve local interests. God became an Anglo-Saxon; an inevitable outcome of the tendency of human beings to manufacture gods after their own likeness. As Voltaire pointed out: "In the beginning God created man in his own image, and, ever since, man has been returning the compliment."

The Englishman related to the world as the arena of empire. His social relations were marked by an effortless superiority, and his identity was centered in simply being an Englishman. It was enough. It was a powerful story and I can remember looking at the enormous globe in grade school and being overawed by the vast areas colored pinky-red to signify those dominions beyond the seas which "belonged" to Great Britain. It was really something to be English!

The American myth, too, is capable of caricature. After the Great War (1914–1918), as England ceased to be "top nation," God began to change nationality and became an American. This was, and is after all, the nation with a "manifest destiny," a destiny anticipated by those early settlers whose theocratic ideas were to mold so much of our present storytelling. "The American Way of Life" was self-evidently superior to all others and it was our destiny to spread this gospel all over the world. Since the anticommunist hysteria of the fifties, the Vietnam debacle of the sixties, and the Watergate revelations of the seventies, the American Dream has suffered terrible wounds. Nevertheless, the United States has much to celebrate. It is a splendid experiment in international and multiracial living. The story, however, needs reworking to embrace the marginal and the outcast—those who were not included in the original plot.

We have ceased to believe in our own mythology, in our own story, precisely because it was not inclusive enough. When a nation loses touch with its story, it loses its identity, and it loses the power which gives life. We also know that as old myths die new ones are being born. It is to be hoped that the emerging story will be a creative, cohesive, and integrating one, one that will embrace all the children of the earth. There are, however, other mythologies which can only be termed devilish.

Such was the Nazi myth. It would be foolish to blame it all on the music of Wagner and the philosophy of Hegel. Nevertheless, Jung has pointed out how much there is of the god Wotan in the rise of National Socialism. Nazism was and is a fantastically successful and powerful story. The fourfold function of a myth is clearly seen. It related man to the mystery behind the universe by identifying that mystery, that *Geist,* with the German people. Secondly, it was believed that the spirit was moving the Germanic spirit into world dominance. Thirdly, the myth united all Nazis into a coherent, effective whole by pinpointing and isolating a common hatred: the Jews. There is nothing like a common enemy, real or imagined, to unite a people. Fourthly, the Nazi could discover his identity by identifying with a movement that transcended his narrow, shrivelled individuality. Alone, he was nothing; as a member of the party, he could stand upright in the world.

One could construct similar disturbing parodies of the Russian and Chinese myths. The great Russian hero was Lenin. It was his genius which forged a new vision out of the crumbling empire of the Tsars. Communism was destined to sweep over all the peoples of the earth, free the enslaved, raise up the poor, and abolish the tyranny of wealth.

The fact that this has not happened does not in any way diminish the magnificence of the vision. The story of Communist China is even more glorious. Mao Tse-tung was both a Moses and a Confucius. Just as the Exodus was the event which forged an undifferentiated rabble escaping from Egypt into a new people, so the "Long March" was the occasion of the forging of a powerful vision of revolution. In spite of his repudiation of Confucius, Mao has emerged as the wise old man of the age whose *Sayings* are designed to replace the *Analects* of Confucius.

Nearer home, we are seeing the inevitable emergence of black and feminist mythologies. These are in direct response to the inadequacies and rigidities of our collective storytelling. Women have figured largely as minor characters, blacks have hardly figured at all. Some elements in these stories are creative, others are patently diabolic. The telling of them is very important. All these myths vie for our attention. These are the power-bearing stories we are telling our children for this generation.

Stories become destructive when they are given divine and absolute status. We tend to divinize those things in the ascendant: the male has had his turn at shooting for divinity, and the female, the black, the poor will not be denied theirs. Justice demands that everyone gets his fair share of the action. In the end, however, we all have to give up our claim to divinity. "Here we have no abiding city" (Heb 13:14). Or, to use Karl Marx's telling aphorism: "Anyone who makes plans for after the revolution is a reactionary."

Nevertheless we are still left with the vexing question of criteria. Is one story as good as another as long as people are foolish enough to believe it? The myth-pusher, like the dope-pusher, can be the herald and cause of destruction. It is by the pusher's storytelling that Jews are annihilated, blacks denied basic rights, women refused an equal place. Men and women of all races and persuasions are pushed under to satisfy the demands of a powerful story. Where are we to find a basis for sound judgment? The Christian people own certain criteria for judging the stories they hear and that dominate our culture. Their criteria are the love and power manifested in the life, death, and resurrection of Jesus Christ. The Christian story liberates us from all other myths and stories, by insisting on the provisional character of all human stories, concepts, and constructs. God and humanity are so met in Christ that human beings share in the hidden and mysterious life of God himself. This gives us an inner life of freedom, of infinite possibilities. The resurrection is the powerful sign of this new life. The other stories in our culture demanding our allegiance lose their binding power because Christ calls everything into question.

We have to unlearn some of the myths and stories which have shaped our thinking. The American needs to unlearn the jingoist's version of his history, to understand that his destiny is not quite so manifest as he thought. The black is already unlearning the inaccuracies of the classroom with regard to his own history. Is it possible for black and white, male and female, to be caught up in a common story of love and freedom? We tend to replace one set of prejudices with another. It is hard for an oppressed group seeing and sharing the wounds of injustice to perceive the flaws in its newly forged myth. It is a painful process. It means letting go of those stories, ideologies, and prejudices which tell us who we are. To lose them would be to lose ourselves. But that is what we must do, not in order to remain lost, but in order to allow new birth and new growth to happen to us. It does not mean we have to abandon everything in our mythical baggage, but rather that we must be prepared to do so if necessary.

Some myths are not incompatible with the Christian story, but what exactly is the Christian story? How do we find out? The Bible can help us if we really read it; the tradition of the Church could help us if we were not (and on good grounds) so suspicious of it. A deeper historical sense would not do us any harm. Where do we begin? Well we have already begun by initiating a process of unlearning and setting foot into the unknown.

There are many myths which are consonant with and illuminate the Christian story: *The Divine Comedy,* the *Legend of the Holy Grail,* and many more. Dante opens his *Divine Comedy* in this way: "In the middle of the road of life, I found myself in a dark wood, where the right way was lost." This is step two of our journey. After the process of unlearning in the wasteland, we have to acknowledge that we are lost and need help. It is then that we begin to learn again. We learn unpleasant things. We begin to understand from the inside what it means to be limited, to be a creature, to be marked for death, to exist in time and space. We realize that all the things for which we work and strive have no lasting value.

Dante meets three beasts in his particular wasteland: the leopard, the lion, and the wolf. All three represent time by which we, who have lost our way, are held, trapped in delusion. The leopard is a sign of the temptations of the flesh: the desire for those things which pass away in time (not, of course, merely sex). The lion is pride, the primal sin, the solipsism by which man, self-bound, is barred from the vision of God, the glimpse of joy. Pride is the refusal to take creatureliness and mortality seriously. We hopelessly take to ourselves the prerogatives of the divine. The wolf is avarice, which is far more than greed for worldly goods; it is a striving for what time takes away. Time takes everything away with it. If we are to journey on we must learn this.

So here at the beginning of our story is an unlearning. We admit that we are lost. We do battle with those beasts which give us only an illusion of permanence. It is a hard road. What did we expect? In the thirteenth-century legend *The Quest for the Holy Grail,* we read that each knight left the fellowship of the Round Table to search for the Holy Grail: "And now each went the way which he had decided, and they set out into the forest at one point or another, *there where they saw it to be the thickest.*" This is exactly our position today, except that the knights of old *chose* to enter the wood where it was thickest. We, on the other hand, have no choice. This is where many of us are.

Which way shall we go? Into a brave atheism? Atheism is a noble path which can help some to think beyond thought, but it is a luxury few can afford. Into madness? Into the lost state of an unhinged mind? This was the fate of that glorious and tormented spirit, Friedrich Nietzsche, who saw reality with a painful clarity. It caused him to lose himself. This brilliant comet of a man burned himself out and collapsed at the height of his powers, at the age of forty-five. From then until his death in 1900, some eleven years later, he remained in a pathetic state of solitariness which only the insane know. It takes a deep form of courage to risk madness. It takes something of the madman's vision to dare to learn from the madman. And we have much to learn.

Paranoia is a word that has entered the popular vocabulary. Literally (although, of course, not technically) it means to be out of your mind. To be paranoid is to have lost your way, like Dante wandering in a land that is far from home. There is another word, which has not yet entered popular speech, for the turning of the mind to the lost home: *metanoia.*

The path of metanoia is a way of glory which leads us home. Paranoia (to be out of your mind) is that process by which the mind is unhinged and the personality splintered and fragmented. Metanoia (to turn the mind, to be in your right mind), which is usually translated in the New Testament as *repentance,* means the restoration of mind, the coming together of the shattered fragments of the self. It means a turning to God as the source and power of life.

Repentance, a permanent revolution of the mind, is the constant stance of the Christian. It is a perpetually turning from death to life. We shrink from this turning because, on the surface, death-bearing time offers the security and comfort of the familiar, the known. Life, on the other hand, always threatens us with the promise of the new.

We shrink from metanoia, from this turning, because we can see that mankind is perpetually engaged in the double activity of going mad and of preventing itself from going mad. This double process consumes all our energy. We go mad in our attempts to control the life which we know will eventually slip through our fingers. We have to surrender, to let go of our hold on life, a hold which we all have to relinquish sooner or later. The secret is that the holding on to life as a possession and its glorious enjoyment are mutually exclusive activities. This is true for the simplest pleasures as for the most sublime relationships. Possessiveness kills enjoyment. Our progress as human beings rests precisely on our accepting this strange circumstance. Real joy requires the free acknowledgement of our helplessness in the face of death.

There are forces in the world and within us which seek to disintegrate the personality. At the same time, there are forces which seek to reduce us by a process of reintegration. This process of turning, of disintegration followed by reintegration, is what Christians call the "madness" of metanoia, of conversion, of being born again.

One such convert, one such "madman" was the great pilgrim, St. Thomas Aquinas. Aquinas, whose *magnum opus* dominated Catholic theology for over six centuries, was forced to enter the wasteland, the dark wood, the painful realm of metanoia. He came through to the other side, and was barely able to tell us something of his vision. One day a great change came over him as he was saying Mass. He had a conversion experience. The Angelic Doctor was struck down by a vision which caused an internal revolution. It was the culmination of his journey into creative "madness." After that Mass he refused to write or dictate another word. He simply and irrevocably gave up his writing. He stopped in the third part of the *Summa,* where he was dealing with the subject of penance. A good place to finish! His fellow schoolmen thought he might be going mad. He hardly spoke: "Everything I have written seems as worthless as straw. . . . Everything I have written seems worthless in comparison with the things I have seen." He died shortly after, on his way to the Council of Lyons, his journey on this side of the grave complete. The monks at the monastery where he died indulged in another form of madness. They were frightened they might lose a precious relic, so they cut off his head and boiled his corpse in order to preserve it!

St. Thomas Aquinas is often represented in Christian iconography as holding a flaming sun in his hand. He clutches it to his breast so that he too burns with light. The sun flames through him. He is a man on fire, an image of the unity of affection and intellect in the intensity of love. In the pedestrian terms of the world, it is a form of madness: to be on fire, to be intoxicated by the transcendent power of the universe which inflames both mind and heart.

The way of Nietzsche and the way of St. Thomas both lead out of the dark wood; one into the madness which is a greater darkness, the other to the glory of a blinding light, a deep but dazzling darkness. Both point to the word which is beyond words. Today the world and the Church need visionaries who will risk creative madness. To share in the divine madness, in the folly of God, who loves his creatures utterly and completely, is our destiny. Such are those who presume to embrace the Christian mystery; they are pioneers in love. We need men and women who risk the creative madness of the love of God so that life will flow through the veins of mankind, so that a frozen world may be warmed back to life, so that the broken may be healed and the dead rise to new life.

We need those who are willing to anticipate and live the future. Some people appear to be called out in each generation to stand in the gateway to the future, to stand right on its edge. They do so, not ideologically but in their own person. There are those who are misplaced, displaced, as signs for our sake of the realities to come.

To be "ahead of one's time" is both a glory and a tragedy. It is a glory because of the vision, it is a tragedy because one has no home, one's time is not yet.

The call to stand in "the gateway to the future" is irresistible, and it works itself out in the individual souls of men and women, in the metaphysical casualties of our generation, in those who are marred by sin and evil for our sake. Some have indeed risked madness and found it to be destructive rather than creative. We need help and guidance through the wasteland.

Joseph Campbell in his essay "Schizophrenia—the Inward Journey,"[3] makes a startling and convincing comparison between the journey of the mystic and that of the schizophrenic. Schizophrenia (loosely speaking) is the condition of one who has withdrawn from life, of one who has lost touch with things. He has no roots and is cut off from himself and other people. From this detached base he enters into the world of his own fantasies. The schizophrenic and the mystic (the former entering the darkness of paranoia and the latter the dazzling darkness of metanoia) have first to break away from their present social environment. They have to go on pilgrimage. There follows a long and deep retreat in which there is a chaotic series of encounters which are dark and terrifying. This is where the mystic and schizophrenic part company. The mystic begins to enjoy encounters of a centering kind which are fulfilling and harmonizing. This pattern of separation, initiation, and return is common to all who make the journey. It parallels the pattern of loss, initiation, and laughter we described earlier. Singing and hilarity have their place, but in due time. To laugh too soon is to laugh vacuously; it is the cackle of insanity.

The mystic and the schizophrenic begin the journey together. Soon vital differences emerge.

> The mystic, endowed with native talents for this sort of thing and following, stage by stage, the instruction of a master, enters the waters and finds he can swim; whereas the schizophrenic, unprepared, unguided, and ungifted, has fallen or

has intentionally plunged, and is drowning. Can he be saved? If a line is thrown to him, will he grab it?[4]

So instruction is necessary if we are not to lose our minds on this journey. We come to our right mind by first finding out from seasoned voyagers something of the wasteland in which we find ourselves. What powers are we likely to encounter? How can they be overcome and their energy redirected? To change the metaphor: With the aid of a guide we enter what appears to be the menacing and turbulent ocean, and much to our joy and surprise, find that we can swim.

Why the images of wasteland and water? Why not ones of a lush meadow in spring sunshine or a safe paddling pool in which we can securely dabble our feet? The wasteland and the ocean speak to us of the strangeness of that truth which is both hidden from us yet within us. We need images that are both familiar and yet contain an element of surprise, of shock, of revelation. We are always living on the edge of some revelation. Something new (and therefore full of hope and terror) is waiting to break us open. Truth lies in ambush for us. It comes to us as a shock because we have no permanent home. Of ourselves, we have no stability. We live with an ever-expanding horizon. What then *is* true?

Truth lies in ambush. The great religions of the world all claim to show us a path through the wasteland, to tell us the secret by which the grotesque may be tamed. They all offer swimming lessons, charts, and maps. They promise a script and scenario for the great drama as it unfolds. All religions have a story to tell. There are, as we might expect, some interesting parallels between Christianity and other religions. Without some knowledge of other religions, Christians will be faced with two dangers. On the one hand, they will be naïvely provincial with regard to Christianity, and on the other they will be blissfully unaware of its startling particularity and disturbing radicalism. We need the nudge of revelation to push us beyond what we know of ourselves. We need the creative shock that will disabuse us of our narrow vision of things.

We need the love of God to be human. We have that love which makes us free.

Shall we go on then through the wasteland, risk lostness, and face Dante's beasts of time? "How shall we sing the Lord's song in a strange land?" (Ps 137:4). Christianity is the vision of life which fools us out of our limits. It is the fathomless deep on which our coracle floats. At first we fight the mystery and, because it is uncontrollable, it appears to us as menacing. Mystery is like the ocean itself. Fight it and we are lost, overcome; relax and accept it and we float. It bears us up and we can begin to sing.

Caedmon (657–680) was a cowherd in the employ of the influential Abbess Hilda of Whitby. At the great communal meals, he used to leave early because he felt useless when the company began to sing and pass around the harp. He had neither voice nor education. One night after he had slipped away he had a dream in which he was called by name and commanded to sing.

The command terrified him. He had been asked to do the very thing he most dreaded. He was brought face to face with his uselessness, his incompetence, and his poverty. In his dream, however, the command was unequivocal: "Sing!" When Caedmon asked what he should sing he was told to sing of the glories of creation. He was told to sing of those things he knew instinctively. Caedmon sang and became the first known poet of Anglo-Saxon England.

Sing of Creation! This is what all the saints have tried to do through the centuries as they went on pilgrimage. Some voices were harsh and discordant, others harmonious and gentle, but the song they sang gave them courage and kept them moving. St. Augustine, in the tenth book of his *Confessions,* sang this way:

> But what is my God? I put my question to the earth. It answered, 'I am not God,' and all things on earth declared the same. I asked the sea and the chasms of the deep and the living things that creep in them, but they answered, 'We are not your God. Seek what is above us.' I spoke to the winds

that blow, and the whole air, and all that lives in it replied, 'Anaximenes is wrong. I am not God.' I asked the sky, the sun, the moon, and the stars, but they told me, 'Neither are we the God whom you seek.' I spoke to all the things that are about me, all that can be admitted by the door of the senses, and I said, 'Since you are not my God, tell me about him. Tell me something of my God.' Clear and loud they answered, 'God is he who made us.'[5]

We are commanded to sing, to begin with the things we know. If all we know now is brokenness and failure we must begin with these. Even these will find a place in the final harmony.

It seems, then, that we are to sing where we are, of what we know; cracked and tuneless as our voice may be, this is what we must do. Even the notes of failure have a place. Yet most of us would prefer to "whistle a happy tune" rather than sing the deeper melody which resonates within us.

All this presents a strange picture, a world in which images and metaphors constantly twist and change. We begin by unlearning; our sense of being cut off makes us cry for help; and finally we are to learn to sing! This pattern is to be found in all religions, in all places, and at all times. We are to begin with the wonder and terror of being itself; the wonder that there is anything at all, the wonder that there is a *you*. That *you* has much to unlearn, much that needs help, and much to sing about.

> In your hands we rest
> In the cup of whose hands sailed an ark
> Rudderless, without mast.
> In your hands we rest
> Who was to make of the aimless wandering of the Ark
> A new beginning for the world.
> In your hands we rest
> Ready and content this day.

4.

The Unlearning of Christianity

THE PLACE OF WAITING

Deserts, dark woods, great journeys, high adventure fill the pages of fairy tale and myth. This is hardly surprising. They are the realm of symbols, of those things which bind up the splintered fragments of reality into some form of coherence. When our symbols deteriorate, so do we. A symbol, no matter how defined, sets limits, gives coherence and a hint of meaning and identity. A wedding ring, a handshake, a kiss are common binding symbols. They speak, in their various ways, of that longing for intimacy which inhabits us all. In friendship and in love it is the touch, flesh to flesh, that gives life. These symbols not only represent relationship, they actually make it.

Each of us, however, has personal symbols, particular icons, which are peculiar to us and are the means by which we make sense of reality: our home, a particular place, a much-loved object. We need such things to stop the chaos breaking in upon us. In time, however, a set of private symbols simply will not do. They may serve to harmonize the realities within but there comes a moment when even our little world seems strange, unfamiliar, and menacing.

Henry Vaughan, in the middle of the seventeenth century, looked deep within himself and found

A peece of much antiquity,
With Hyerogliphicks quite dismembered,
And broken letters scarce remembered,
I tooke them up, and (much Joy'd) went about
T'unite those peeces, hoping to find out
The mystery; but this neer done
That little light I had was gone.[6]

When we dare look within ourselves there is glory and wonder, but it is a dismembered glory, a scarce-remembered wonder. Things do not hang together as they should. The symbols we once treasured lose their power to heal and to save. So it is when a long love grows cold, a cherished belief suddenly dies.

Sometimes there is no explaining it. It is like those disappointing, nostalgic trips back to the scenes of childhood. *Then* everything, including the grown-ups, seemed to be larger than life, and full of wonder: *now* the adults have shrunk along with the architecture and furnishings. For no apparent reason the window through which we perceive reality is suddenly cracked and cloudy. Our vision fades along with the magic that used to permeate our existence. The mirror is shattered, the light fades, the interpretive symbols lose their charm, and we are alone.

The icon (our overarching picture of reality) soon degenerates into an idol which needs to be smashed. Creative iconoclasm is the breaking of idols to release the old power trapped within them. We ask ourselves what was the basic and devastating experience in mankind that gave rise to the symbol in the beginning? It is then that we must reaffirm those primal realities which first called forth the symbols and which open up a way for glory and wonder. The idol is broken only to make way for the icon, the life-bearer. Genuine symbols bear witness to a genuine life. Whatever our symbols are to be they must reflect and mediate the awe-fulness and glory of meaning and of death. So many of our popular symbols avoid both.

For Christians the supreme icon is the cross of Christ in which the lostness of mankind and the love and glory of God are joined in the resurrection. It stands in direct contradiction to the success-promising symbols in the culture: the house, the car, the robust sexual life, the persistent cheating of the final enemy—death. The cross is a shocking and blasphemous symbol in a success-oriented world. It is a sign of the brokenness and vulnerability of God. It is a token of his hiddenness and of his love. At Golgotha we can see that the tree of Eden and the tree of Calvary are one. Life comes out of death. The key to our myth, our personal and collective destiny, is the cross. Have we not forgotten that simple but revolutionary fact? The cross is a saving icon, an effective symbol. It is not only to be gazed upon but to be acted upon, appropriated, lived. The cross of Christ accomplishes something. In fact it accomplishes everything, for it is here that the great mystery, unifying all opposites, resides. Ours is a journey into the heart of that mystery.

It is difficult to see how anyone living in the world today could ignore existence as cruciform. This century has had its share of human tragedy and evil. The cross binds us together as human beings. There is solidarity in sin! The cross is the supreme place where Christ identifies with our humanity, with our mortality. There is a strangely comforting solidarity in the human condition. We are consubstantial. We human beings are made of the same stuff. Reality is something shared. If there is solidarity in sin, there is also solidarity in glory. In a shrinking world we are beginning to realize that all humanity has a common destiny. In the global village reality is convivial because we are all on the same journey. We are all pilgrims.

The journey is a communal one. We do not travel alone even though we are often consumed by loneliness. Our physical, psychic, and spiritual life is bound up with others. One of the lessons of living a common life is the unavoidable connection that is made between individualism and death. We journey together or not at all. To imagine we can make it alone is absurd. We really are all in the same boat, in the same ark. Mankind shares a common destiny. We, in our pathetic determination to be individualistic, have repressed this fact. Individualism is the bedfellow of a living death. Genuine life, on the other hand, is essentially communal and cohabits with such unpopular things as duty, service, and social responsibility. Is that the way we must journey, shackled to words like "duty" and "service"? Where are "the cakes and ale"?

The "cakes and ale" are the gifts of a true individuality. To deny individualism (rugged or otherwise) is not to deny individuality. An open and free community of freed individuals is one definition of the heavenly Jerusalem. The description is a trifle prosaic but nevertheless true: that the creation of such an open and freeing community will depend on the telling of stories and the penetration of symbols. It will call for a self-surrender, a self-donation on our part.

There is within each one of us a battle between the shriveled and fragmented self we are at present and the wider self which is battling to be. There is a war between our chronic individualism and our nascent individuality with its larger sense of oneness with all that is. There is, even in the middle of our struggle for identity, the presence of wine and laughter. "Identity crisis" has now passed into our platitudinous cliché-ridden vocabulary. It has become something of a joke. People who know something of the voyage ahead are unlikely to be terrified by such crises. They are, after all, expected. There is nothing peculiar about having an identity crisis, since it, like death, comes as part of our humanity. The issue is *how* are we to handle the crisis already present.

The Eastern mind solves this problem by insisting that "identity" is an illusion anyway; there is, in reality, no differentiation between the individual and the world. Even the journey is illusion. Identity presupposes differentiation—I am this and not that. The world of multiplicity is an illusion. The secret is the annihilation of the ego. Thus the Eastern mind can say, not that "I am united with the eternal," but that "I *am* the eternal," since there is only the one reality. The Christian asserts (as I suspect many Easterners would) the double affirmation: *"This* is thou—*neither* is this thou."

I am who I am and yet there is a "me" that is not yet. A tree is alive with divinity and is nevertheless not divine. It is the apparent contradiction which trips up the neat and tidy mind. We have an identity and yet it is unformed and unfinished. The Christian expresses this mystery by asserting that his identity (who he really is) is hidden with Christ in God, and that the path back "home" to his true self involves the giving up of that fragment he calls his "self."

Depth psychology has done much to illuminate the path back to a full humanity. In the language of the Christian pilgrimage, we are on our way to "being" in all its fullness of glory. Depth psychology uses the ambiguous words "self" and "Self" to describe this pilgrimage. The freed and freeing life, always open to the future, is *life in the spirit.* The spiritual life is that life which fosters the making of those creative connections which form our sense of identity. The spiritual life is a pattern of relatedness, connectedness, and conviviality by which we know our place in God, in the world, with regard to others, and with regard to our inner development. As we allow the symbols to vibrate within us, our prayers, our eucharists, push us deeper into the exploration of our identity. Sometimes it is the very tediousness of prayer, its basic given rhythm which goads us on and reminds us of the infinite possibilities of an open future. We are granted a glimpse of joy. The symbols of broken bread and wine outpoured will, if we allow them to work within us, be sufficient food for the journey. The Eucharist provides food for travelers, for those on pilgrimage, for those on their way home.

Our repeated rituals meet our need for continuity, for order, for connectedness. But we are not very good at repeating the same thing week after week, day after day. The power of the symbols dries up. We get bored. Yet it is in repeated ritual acts that a people find their identity in the rehearsal of a common story, and thus share in a common hope. We easily forget our roots. We have a poor memory. Christian ritual is the repeated unmasking of men and women before the living mystery of God. It is a ritual dying and a ritual recreation of the believer. Rituals are those dramatic liturgical events which carry us through the crises and major turning points on our journey from birth to death.

The erosion of Christian symbolism and the impoverishment of ritual has been sadly documented in the perennial and now worn out battle between Catholicism and Protestantism. As Jung pointed out some time ago when writing about the collective unconscious, the history of Protestantism, seen from one point of view, is that of a chronic if brave iconoclasm. From the Reformation onward the old symbols were eroded or destroyed. The Protestant principle strode through the powerful symbols of Catholicism like one of Cromwell's Independent Roundheads, smashing images, breaking down idols, stabling the horse in the holy of holies —all in zeal for the Lord of Hosts. As Cromwell was bent on destroying the Catholic myth, he was creating his own. We can admire such a man but we can never love him. He has left us impoverished. We seek those images that once gave life to so many. Even as we unearth them we know it is too late and, in our restlessness, we turn frantically and fashionably to the images of the East. Jung was convinced that this growing impoverishment of symbol has a meaning, and he warned against our covering our spiritual nakedness with borrowed finery. Better to endure our spiritual poverty than lay claim to treasures which do not rightly belong to us. Our heritage in the West consists of those symbols forged out of Judeo-Christian experience. Yet we have squandered our treasure, trampled it underfoot. We are sadly ignorant of those things that lie buried in our own storehouse while we amateurishly try to ransack someone else's.

Must we live in a symbol-less, image-less age? Is the ark really rudderless? Will the ocean swallow us up? The Protestant, says Jung, has to live in this poverty. The Catholic, on the other hand, has all the symbols he needs. There is a superabundance of them. There is only one problem. The symbols are there, but they have died; there is no life in them. Both Catholic and Protestant (indeed religious people in general) long for security and certainty in a shifting and changing world. There is always the temptation to opt for an unreflective and undisturbed form of piety. The desire for a haven of peace causes many to treat their Church as a womb from which (they note) they will never have to emerge. For Christians, those who have been buried with Christ in baptism, this fetal approach to reality is disastrous. To "die with Christ" is to live in a world where everything is in question. This, after all, is the liberty promised us in the Gospel. By holding on to Christ, the Christian can let go of everything else! Indeed, it is getting more and more difficult to remain a fetal Christian. The pressure toward birth is reaching a climax in the Western Church, and one wonders what will be born. We who are about to die demand a miracle!

Like the old Reformation, the new one is also iconoclastic; only this time icons are less plentiful. The choice seems to be either to live with no symbols at all or to live (if you call it living!) with symbols long dead. The journey still beckons, but what if it leads nowhere? Before the symbols passed away we at least had the hope of "journeys end in lovers' meeting." We live with the contradiction. History, anthropology, theology, the whole accumulative evidence of millennia, point to the fact that we cannot live without story and symbol, without that which gives who and what we are some promise of integrity and coherence. The journey itself is a symbol, and one which is impossible to evade. Our willingness to enter the world of the symbolic journey is the means by which the aimless wanderings of the ark can be transformed into a new beginning. The desert, the ocean, images of broken symbols and distorted icons, can be seen in and by a new light. Is it possible for us, in the silence, to recapture, be recaptured by, the God who was in Christ? To see, really see, the mighty crucifix for what it is, the secret of the universe, the music of the spheres, the rhythm of every human heart?

We need to walk by the light of Christ, by the power of the word of God which is given to us without the threat of coercive authority. It is a doctrine without the benefit of prestige and power. It enjoys only a crucified strength. Christology is *the* dogma which releases us from the power of all dogma. Any belief coercively imposed is doomed. We have been too long in the wasteland of a coercive, moralistic Christianity: *Roma locuta: causa finita.* (Rome has spoken: the matter is closed.) To Rome we could add other cities: Geneva and Canterbury, for example. And in the political sphere there are still the voices of Washington, Moscow, and Peking. Perhaps we are less openly coercive now than in the Middle Ages, but we are no less Procrustean. Procrustes had an iron bed and, no matter how tall or short his unwilling guests were, they were made to fit it: either by stretching or by amputation. Procrustes, the patron saint of conformity, still lives. We would rather have the slavery of religion and ideology than the freedom of the Gospel. We are the all-too-willing conspirators in our own enslavement.

The Christian myth has, by and large, been shaped by an authoritarian *ecclesia docens* (the Church teaching) dictating to a passive *ecclesia docta* (the Church taught), and somewhere between the two, the symbols have been lost and we unskilled travelers have been left abandoned. We have rightly reacted against the mindless bleating of such phrases as "the Church teaches" or "tradition demands" because these things in themselves have no life in them. The Church, of course, does have a great deal to teach. And tradition can make legitimate demands on us, but not in a bullying or coercive way. This, to use a popular term, is not the Christian style. Symbols simply *are.* They are neither created nor destroyed by human fiat. One such given symbol, for us, is that of the broken king hanging on the cross.

God reveals himself in all his glory on the cross: in foolishness, in weakness, in brokenness. This strange power of God shows up our human power for what it truly is: utter bankruptcy. The tradition of the crucified God, rightly understood, proclaims that the secret of our living is in our letting go of life. Tradition is the handing on of life. Even the dedicated revolutionary cannot escape tradition. There is no way we can get hold of the new except by tools forged in the past. The living tradition invites us to state afresh the Gospel of life. Otherwise, the most living of all things becomes the most deadly.

Tradition is the Christian story told and retold. It is, in reality, a principle of growth. When the cross degenerates into the plastic crucifix, the Church and its tradition have no hold on us. Indeed, they are empty shells devoid of life, the enemy of art, poetry, and adventure. Everything is petrified by the Medusa stare of misunderstood doctrine, by the repetition of half-remembered glory, by the incoherent mumbling of the faithful of what was once the word of life.

When Christians participate in this self-contradiction, then their myths and rites, their grasp of history as the theater of God's activity, become deadening and deadly because the faith they proclaim is unrelated to actual needs, to the experiences and potentialities of men and women.

A vigorous, disciplined, free, pioneering Christian life is possible. Not because we are wiser than our fathers but because the Gospel is always breaking out of the cell in which we have imprisoned it and coming to us as a free gift. We must learn to journey through places where, in love, ultimate questions are always raisable; places of unfreezing, of thawing, to allow blood to flow, springs to revive, rivers to come crashing down to water the desert places. Where are these places? They are deep within ourselves waiting to be uncovered.

Today these mythic, deeper rhythms of life are being rediscovered. Where there is promise of new life there is always danger. The pitfalls are superabundant. We are a people hungry for meaning. America might be called the "Land of a Thousand Sects." It is not that we are skeptical (would that we were!), but rather that we are so hungry for belief that we will swallow anything. There are many in this world, wearing the rags of old mythologies, who would, for a price, lead us into the promised land. As we have seen, there are myth-pushers as well as dope-pushers in our culture, and they bring in their wake the dangerous assumption that the mythological, symbolic undestanding of existence militates against our reason, against rationality.

To make the journey does not mean leaving the mind behind. Nothing could be more dangerous than the movement toward anti-intellectualism. A detached pseudomystical approach can allow people to commit evil with equanimity. The mind is not all there is, but we dare not deny it place and value. We are creatures of the word and words. Even as they slip and slide, they should make sense. Humanly speaking, we come to a glimpse of the truth by a process of dialectic. The method is one of a dialogue in which no one has the last word, no one has a monopoly on truth, no one has God or the meaning of things buttoned up. This is a heady and refreshing thought, though one which very few are able to live with because it does mean abandoning old securities.

This is why we must wait in the darkness. We must wait, we must be still in order to allow mystery once again to penetrate that deep dark place that exists in all of us: the mystery of a unity of body, mind, and spirit. Waiting is a terrifying and wonderful activity because it involves our facing a profound disorder within ourselves. There is not the harmony of body, mind, and spirit, which is necessary for wholeness. It is as if we have to navigate the waters of the deep without chart or compass.

It is impossible for us to gaze steadily at the noonday sun. To gaze steadily into the darkness within is almost beyond our endurance. The dangers are twofold. Our first impulse is to attack the impenetrability of mystery by reasoning it out. We would rather have the comforting beams of a false light than no light at all. The opposite temptation, as we have said, is equally dangerous: to lapse into a lazy, yet dogmatic, anti-intellectualism. This latter temptation is invidious because it tries to make mystery the ultimate "explanation." "Ah, but that's a mystery," we say, and imagine that we have said something significant.

We are not to idolize the intellect nor are we to abandon it with regard to this darkness. Rather, we are to *enter* the mystery which is both within us and beyond us. When we wait, when we are still, we come to see the "as if" of our fearful navigation of the deep. It is only "as if" we have no chart or compass. A voice does answer our call *de profundis.* There are, after all, the means of navigation. We then nervously begin to navigate by sun and stars. The Christian learns to navigate by Christ. Christ known as the one who knows us more than we know ourselves; Christ encountered in the story, living for us in the Bible; Christ broken and poured out in bread and wine; Christ seen in the eyes of everyone we meet. Christianity is not a comforting explanation of mystery. It is a voyage into it. Christ is a person, *the* person, to be encountered, not a puzzle which we would rather ignore. The Christian creeds were never meant to be explanations of the mystery of Christ. They are invitations to adventure. They demand hard thinking; they do not obliterate the necessity of intellectual exercise. They are the first word, not the last word, with regard to the Christian way. They are springboards into awe and wonder, not their denial.

By far the best version of the creed is not *Credo in Unum Deum* but *Te Deum Laudamus:* We praise thee, O God. Praise, adoration, is the only appropriate posture we can adopt as we wait and are still in the darkness. In an attitude of adoration, this darkness begins to dazzle and we catch a glimpse of what intensity of light there must be to cause such a scintillating darkness.

If we are to survive, then, on this journey, we are to use our heads as well as our hearts, to seek to understand who and what we are, who and what we celebrate; to discern the word beyond mere words. We are to use our reason to the full, and at the same time acknowledge its fearful limitations. As I sit now at my desk, I live with the absurd thought that I am dust—glorious, impossible dust —and that time is short.

What, then, is demanded of me? Must I grit my teeth and bravely endure the meaninglessness of everything? Does the meaning of life lie in the paradoxical (or is it nonsensical?) discovery that life has no meaning? This is one way to interpret the baffling reality of the world. Another way, no less demanding, leads us away from this kind of hopelessness into a position where hope is also a reality. Rather than grapple with the tiger of despair as we all spiral downward into the abyss of meaninglessness, we can learn in the mystery of our chronic incapacity to grasp the unconditional enormity of the meaning offered us. "The fault, dear Brutus, is not in the stars but in ourselves." The root of the problem lies in our smallness, in our incapacity to catch a glimpse of the meaning of the universe in rational terms.

Truth, in the end, is not something we grasp but something which grasps us. It grasps us, takes hold of us, transfigures us by the means of life-giving symbols, often coming to us in story form.

The great Anglican theologian Austin Farrer did much to revive the life-giving symbols of Christianity. He pointed out many years ago that images have a direct epistemological function. Epistemology is that branch of philosophy which investigates the origin, nature, methods, and limits of human knowledge. We can *know* certain things only by means of poetry, myth, and symbol. That is to say, they tell us of things which cannot be told in any other way. They illuminate us directly, without the intervention of an intermediate state of conceptual thought. For example, the image of hell in Dante presents us with a picture of the deepening possibilities of evil within the soul in a way that no academic treatise could. As the soul goes deeper into hell, the images change from fire and flame into those of snow and ice. Think of the image of ice. Ice causes a deeper pain than fire. To use an image from the fairytale *The Snow Queen,* there is, within the human heart, a splinter of deadening ice which has to be melted before love can return.

Dante knew of the terrible "conjunction of opposites" within the human heart: fire and ice. The imagery of his poetry communicates things to us on a deeper level than formal thought. As such, it is the giver of life. In what other form could Dante's piercing vision come to us? We need to be bombarded with life-bearing images which go deeper than logic. There we may find the word beyond words, in everyday things, in the patterns given to us by our very existence, in our birth, in our growth, in our sexuality, and in our dying. It is to these we must now turn, if we are to continue our journey.

5.

Being Born Again

THE JOURNEY BEGINS

There was one of the Pharisees named Nicodemus, a member of the Jewish Council, who came to Jesus by night. "Rabbi," he said, "we know that you are a teacher sent by God; no one could perform these signs of yours unless God were with him." Jesus answered, "In truth, in very truth I tell you, unless a man has been born over again he cannot see the kingdom of God." "But how is it possible," said Nicodemus, "for a man to be born when he is old? Can he enter his mother's womb a second time and be born?" Jesus answered, "In truth I tell you, no one can enter the kingdom of God without being born from water and spirit. Flesh can give birth only to flesh; it is spirit that gives birth to spirit. You ought not to be astonished, then, when I tell you that you must be born over again. The wind blows where it wills; you hear the sound of it, but you do not know where it comes from, or where it is going. So with everyone who is born from spirit."

John 3:1–8

We have surveyed the landscape, taken our bearings, gathered together the fragments of a map, and faced the strange possibilities of the impending journey. Now it is time to begin in earnest. Birth, new birth, is the logical and inescapable place to start. The initiates in every religion have to be "born again," and the imagery of new birth is pervasive throughout the sacred literature of the great religions. In the mind of man, birth, the darkness of the womb, is inextricably bound up with another birth, the darkness of death itself. The journey from birth to death is depicted in mythology and in literature as an adventure, a voyage from one darkness to another, from one womb to another place of gestation. There are between the moment of actual birth and actual death, many other births and deaths. It is not always easy for us to distinguish between a moment of dying and a moment of new birth. The womb of the new life is often identical with the tomb of the old.

In psychological terms the trauma of birth is of the utmost importance in determining subsequent growth and development. Initiation rites, both secular and religious, involve a ritualistic return to the womb to await a new birth. This being born again means being born *into* a community, a fellowship. It also involves a new relationship with parental figures and both parents can be experienced as either nurturing or menacing.

Being born, being thrust from the womb in a moment of violent exaltation, is the first thing imprinted upon us. It affects us as persons, psychologically and spiritually. It is the birth trauma, which is the fundamental source for much of our mythology and theology. Being present for the birth of our second daughter, I was struck by two things (which no doubt I should have expected): the speed and the violence of Charlotte's birth. Perhaps violence is not the right word: eagerness, impatience, yearning? Charlotte appeared to be fighting for a place in the light of day and yet violently objecting all the way. It is a wonder we ever recover from being born! Some of us, perhaps, never have been born, except physically. Like the baby in the womb, we fight to be born and not to be born again at the same time. What we want most we avoid most. So it is that we resist and yet embrace every pressure toward rebirth. We resist and assist that first violent step of the way. We tend to move from one womb into another. The world itself is a womb; Holy Mother Church, *(Sancta Mater Ecclesia),* the Communist Party, America the Beautiful—all are womblike.

As the critic Cyril Connolly put it: "We are looking for a womb with a view." a place where we are safe and secure. We all have to be born again, not once but many times if we are to enter the kingdom. This deep longing for growth was and is the central force in the Christian pilgrimage. The Christian is always being born anew. The pressure to grow is inherent and yet we fight it. Hence the Christian life is neither simple nor easy. We ache for related-ness, for belonging, which brings us into the Church (and if not *the* Church, then *a* Church of our own making). We reach out toward meaning, and faith's name for that meaning is God. There is a self within each one of us aching to be born, a self burdened with contradiction, and everything (I mean *everything*) we do is designed to alleviate the discomfort caused by contrary forces within us. George Herbert, priest and poet of the seventeenth century, revealed that even someone of his aristocratic background and steady Anglican belief could suffer the pains of a turbulent, pregnant spirit:

> Ah my deare Father, ease my smart!
> The contrarieties crush me: these crosse actions
> Do winde a rope about and cut my heart:
> And yet since these thy contradictions
> Are properly a crosse felt by thy sonne,
> With but foure words, my words, Thy will be done.[7]

Contrarieties crush us. We, like the heroes of old, have to enter a mythological cycle of descent and return, of death and resurrec-tion. Unless some of us are willing to make the journey, I see little hope for the Church, for the world, for all those things that make genuine humanity at least a possibility. Without such pioneers, however reluctant they may be, there is no glimpse of real joy.

Herbert knew the pain of aimless wanderings. His real journey only began after he had left behind the promise of a glittering career at court or university and had settled into the obscure life of his little parish at Bemerton. Only then were his wanderings transformed into a journey home.

My crooked winding ways wherein I live—
Wherein I die not live—for life is straight
Straight as a line that ever tends to thee.[8]

As far as the real journey is concerned, Herbert was a hero in the grand manner in spite of the fact that on the surface his life was unspectacular.

The hero in mythology goes on a journey and comes through at the end with a special gift, a cure for some ill, or an elixir. The hero of the seminal Jewish myth is Moses, the midwife of a great nation. Moses experienced rebirth at the burning bush (Ex 3:1–6); he gained direct knowledge of the *mysterium tremendum* and, under the impetus of Yahweh, he assisted at the birth of a new nation, the Chosen People. They became a people with a destiny to enter the Promised Land after their baptism in the Red Sea. The three-fold pattern is discernible throughout the pages of history: a hero, a new people, a destiny. There is, even to the most jaded and cynical of us, something Mosaic about the founders of this nation and the subsequent history of the United States, in the whoring after other gods, that is not dissimilar to that of ancient Israel. This Mosaic pattern is impressed upon the Christian at baptism. He is buried with Christ in the waters of baptism, is dead and rises to new life in Christ.

There is, however, one problem. As far as the Mosaic understanding of reality goes, the individual's relationship to God depends entirely on his being a member of a community. We are not born in a vacuum, nor do we journey entirely alone (although loneliness is often part of the burden). Being reborn, being made alive, involves being born into a community. So there are strings attached to this adventure. Far from being the spiritual journey of the solitary individual in search of God, it drags a people, a church, a nation, the human race, along with it. Being reborn, touched and quickened by God, does not seem such a good idea after all. As the Old Testament shows in the writings of the prophets (Moses, Jeremiah, Hosea, Amos), it is a doubtful privilege to be the elect of

God. It is better, surely, to stay in the warm, wet, dark womb than to step out into these realities and risk madness. We have been warned, after all, what to expect. Not only do we have the fantastic accumulative witness of human history, but we have hidden deep within ourselves the imprint of our first birth, with its trauma, its violence, the attendant loss of security and the threat of death.

The loss of security and the threat of death (if movies and plays are anything to go by) linger on throughout the thing we call life. As Kazantzakis' Zorba says: "Life is what you do while you are waiting for death." Everything conspires to push us deeper into darkness and make us less human. In California there is a housing development which designs your house—or rather your womb— down to the ashtrays and tea towels. One has a choice of styles, even in the paintings: seascapes, country scenes, or modern. The burden of choice here is removed, and as each burden is taken off our shoulders, so too is lessened the possibility that the planet can remain human. Remove the burden of freedom, remove that pressure to go on a voyage, and the forces of darkness take over.

We know from studies in child psychology that this trauma of birth has to be relived around age three. The child regresses, tries to go back to being a tiny baby, and cannot. It is by a process of reliving his birth and early infancy that he is able to let it go and continue the painful and glorious process of becoming a person. At various stages in our lives we resist the pressure to be born again, we refuse freedom. There is a very funny, yet disturbing, Charles Addams cartoon: two women are looking at an enormous blob sitting in an armchair. The only sign of life are its beady eyes. One woman is turning to the other, saying: "We're still waiting for Stanley to jell." Some of us have yielded up all responsibility, all choice, all initiative. We have refused our freedom and become "blobs" destined never to jell. We turn our backs on rites of initiation.

The imprint of birth in primitive religions was reenacted at the time of puberty during the initiation rites, the rites of reentry into the womb to await a yet more violent birth. The ancient knight prostrated himself before the altar on which his sword was to be consecrated, prepared himself for the quest by a long vigil in the darkness. (How feeble the Church's sacrament of confirmation is in this context!)

In the Christian scheme of things, contrition is a prerequisite for this journey, this process. In the early Church, each confession was seen as a quasi-deathbed confession which signified a new birth, a fresh start, a beginning again. Indeed this sacrament was called the Mystery of the Second Baptism. Contrition was the means by which the penitent was pushed into a new life. Contrition is precisely the free acceptance of the pangs of new birth. It is the willingness to be broken up, to accept and welcome the penetrating light, that really matters. We have to be prepared to allow our stiff, enameled complacency, which seeks to present an unbroken front, to be pierced and in the end destroyed.

Now, it is a glorious wonder to contemplate, to see with our full being the historic story which brought and keeps the Church in being. To share its glory and its mystery, to explore it, to voyage within it, we need to see, to contemplate. Richard of St. Victor defined contemplation as "the clear gaze of a free spirit, suspended in wonder, on the marvels of wisdom." "The clear gaze of a free spirit" is hard and painful to maintain. We can no more do it than we can gaze at the noonday sun. These are hard truths to contemplate.

What, after birth, are we to gaze upon on our voyage? If we are to be true to our pattern, after that first stage comes the second "mother." Mother has had, to say the least, a bad press ever since the Oedipus-Freud alliance. The image of man (male) being mothered and smothered to death is all too familiar in our culture. The breast, symbol of glorious symbiosis, tells us (according to the psychologist Piaget) that mother is the universe and, when mother is absent, so is the universe. So mother is, from the beginning, a source of deep bliss and happiness and, because of her possible absence, a source of danger, separation, and terrible destruction. This sense of terror and wonder continues to operate in that vast treasury of our subconscious. In this enormous storehouse everyone we encounter who is in a position of authority is shaped by this parental imprint. Father figures belong, however, not to the preverbal world of infancy but to the world of the already talking infant. Mother is there right from the beginning. So father figures and mother figures, while both operating powerfully in the subconscious, do so on different levels. Mother goes much deeper; and, because her influence prevails over the child from birth, she is a much more mysterious figure.

The myth of the great journey is one of the ways human beings of both sexes compensate for the great mother's deep and pervading influence. We must free ourselves from her if we are to grow. Now, when we talk of the mother figure, it is important for us to understand that we are not talking of *particular* mothers or of women in general. We are talking of a powerful mother symbol which a nurturing-devouring male could also incarnate. The mother figure in myth and symbol is experienced both positively, as warm and protective, and negatively, as possessive and destructive.

There is a great temptation nowadays to confuse sexual imagery with gender. We would do well to watch out for father figures. They are just as dangerous as mother figures. The love of the mother is freely given. One does not have to earn or deserve it. Yet it is a love that can consume. The love of the father, on the other hand, has to be earned. He is never satisfied.

The great error in the ancient Christian ascetical tradition was to locate the problem and source of sin in Eve's sexuality. This is sheer, if understandable, evasion, and we have managed to sustain this evasion. Genesis says that Eve is "the *mother* of all living" (Gen 3:20). It is no accident that the cult of the great mother is the most archaic and pervasive of all forms of religion. Dare we admit that the deepest religious urge within us all today is still to succumb to her engulfing arms and appease her hunger? Religions, in their destructive form, appear to fluctuate between allegiance to the devouring mother and obedience to the angry father. The parodies of Christianity and Judaism belong to the latter class.

We must leave mother behind in all her powerful, luminous and pervasive forms. Just as we have, on the journey, to leave the womb, so we have to leave mother, the one who gave us birth. Wombless and motherless, we are struck with the fearsome givenness of things, the *isness* of life (the *Istigkeit* of Meister Eckhart). The *isness* often oppresses us. We feel hemmed in by the limitations of time and space. We feel that there is no freedom, only fate.

You are *here* at *this* time and in *this* place. Why? How far each one of us has traveled God only knows; no doubt we long not to be mediocre, accidental, or mortal. But we are all three, and the truth of this is actually maddening. We nurse within our hearts the hope that we are different, that we are special, that we are extraordinary. We long for the assurance that our birth was no accident, that a god had a hand in our coming to be, that we exist by divine fiat. We ache for a cure to the ultimate disease of our mortality, for a way to cheat death, for the medicine of immortality. Our madness comes when the pressure is too great and we fabricate a vital lie to cover up the fact that we are mediocre, accidental, mortal. We fail to see the glory of the Good News. The vital lie is unnecessary because all the things we truly long for have been freely given to us.

We wish we had never embarked on this voyage. What passes for our so-called mystical journey is an escape back to the womb, home to mother. We seek a form of immortality by trying to crawl back into the cosmic egg, to eat the flowery food of the lotus, to go back into warm death, to seek escape in exercises, in elixirs. It is like grasping at the wind. It is like trying to talk to a photograph of a person instead of face to face. There is no road to immortality save through the "contrarieties" of death and resurrection; no short cut to meaning, no philosopher's stone to turn our lead into gold.

There is a story of a Chinese emperor who ordered his wise men to manufacture immortality pills for him. He died of an overdose.

We are like his imperial majesty as we resist going on the journey, and as we seek short cuts to life everlasting.

One short cut is by the way of experience. This is an age in which people are understandably desperate for experience. Experience is just as dangerous as the web which is woven around the mystery. Experience can be a drug, which, in the end, destroys or obscures the very reality that gave rise to the experience. We stagger from experience to experience: each time needing a larger shot of it than the last. Worse: we tend to bully and coerce others with our experiences. "If you would be saved then you must duplicate my experience of reality." When we have been granted a vision we wish it to be reproduced in everyone we meet.

When we are granted a vision there is a great danger of what psychologists call "inflation." We tend to suffer from megalomania. Since we are fresh from our peculiar vision, we often believe we have a special knowledge not granted to other mortals. This is the danger of all so-called mystical experience.

It is dangerous because everything is made to serve the experience, which becomes the sole criterion by which everything else is judged. The danger can be avoided if the mystical voyager keeps hold of one very important distinction: that of the difference between himself and his experience. The fourteenth-century anonymous mystic and teacher, usually called simply the author of *The Cloud of Unknowing,* made this distinction clear when he wrote concerning the union of the soul with God in contemplation: "For he is your being, and you are what you are in him . . . preserving always this difference between you and him, that he is your being and that you are *not* his."

To those who are given some mystical experience, there is never any justification for pride, for self-glorification, for inflation. We are bearers of God. We are not God. There have been those who have claimed divinity for themselves and this is a peculiar kind of madness which hinges on a half-truth. Mankind, on the whole, has wisely been skeptical concerning mystics and mystical experience. The pages of history have been ripped and torn by inflated persons.

In this sense both Caligula and Hitler were mystics: god-filled, inflated. Some have seen themselves not merely as *a* savior of mankind (which they may well be) but as *the* Savior, not merely as a mother but *the* great mother of us all. When such inflation occurs, a destructive madness is let loose upon the world.

The death of the self, which would deify its own visions and experiences, is one way of understanding the mystery of Christian baptism. It is the sacrament of new birth which involves a continual dying to the old self and its past experiences.

The womb, if we stay too long, does become a tomb from which we will never emerge. We shall have to return to the mystery of sexuality and the struggle for sexual identity, but we must first look at the third imprint which shaped and shapes our mythologies. According to anthropologists and psychologists, after the womb and mother comes the imprint associated with excrement.

6.

The Journey Fails

THE SENSE OF SIN AND DEFILEMENT

After birth and mother comes the powerful image of excrement. This third imprint colors our attitudes to all that is. It speaks of filth, guilt, sin, that which is forbidden. There is a dark part of us which we deem unseemly and even vile, a lurking horror which we dare not mention.

At about two-and-a-half, children are fascinated by their "productions" and, indeed, take pride in them. It is a creative act, a thing of value, suitable even as a gift, until someone tells the child it is something forbidden, filthy, "icky," darkly unpleasant. In the child's mind a dualism springs up. There enters into his life the unmentionable side of existence.

This side of existence has been ably and devastatingly documented by modern psychiatry. It might be as well, here, for me to acknowledge my debt to the depth psychologists and to Jung in particular.

The work of Carl Jung, above all others, has done much to restore "religion" to its rightful place in the life of humanity. That rightful place is at the center of human life as its fount and origin. In many ways Jung has done his job too well. It is difficult to admire him and yet resist the temptation to interpret the whole of reality in Jungian terms. Jung was a brave and fearless explorer of human consciousness. He was not the founder of a school of disciples. Disciples never get it quite right; they deify the master who never entertained any claims for divinity. The apotheosis of Jung can do a great deal of harm. There is the temptation to interpret the Gospel merely in Jungian terms, whereas there is a sense in which the Gospel is that which judges and interprets Jung. Some have fallen into the trap of "psychologism." Psychologism is the attempt to explain all experience in psychological terms. Thus, the "Christian Jungian" who is intent on seeing Christ unfold within himself as he progresses toward self-fulfillment, or individuation, is often blinded to the possibility that there may be dimensions to explore other than the narrowly psychological. There is a tendency in psychologism to neglect the possible metaphysical or supernatural grounds of spiritual experience. I do not believe Jung fell into this trap himself. Suffice it to say I find Jung enormously helpful, not so much for his particular doctrines but rather for the relentless honesty with which he pursued them. Jung revealed the "unmentionable side" of life to be not only a place of horror but also one of daring creativity and vitality.

He records one of his dreams of early childhood. It was a dream which he tried many times to repress. On each occasion, he was overcome with a sense of foreboding and dread. Such awful thoughts could not be tolerated by his conscious mind. One day the impulse was too great and he dreamed his dream: there before him was a beautiful cathedral, glittering with the rich panoply of the liturgy. Above the cathedral sat the Lord God defecating on the whole proceedings!

For Jung this was an unthinkable thing that forced itself to be thought. Yet it was precisely this dream that released in him spiritual energies which enabled him to journey deep into the meaning of things. We all realize there is a dark side to our nature about which we know, or pretend to know, very little. We know that certain things simply are not done: "We don't do that sort of thing in our family." There is a myriad of taboos, unwritten laws, inhibiting legislation, which weave their labyrinthine pattern round our lives and prevent us from embarking on the voyage that is vital for us to make if we are to live.

Jung's experience after his dreadful dream was one of release, freedom, sheer grace. The only action possible for someone who has dared this far on the journey is an act of faith. This is especially true of those of us who claim to be "religious." To grasp the full absurdity of vocation is to have dared to think the unthinkable. We are *not* what we say we are. A human being is a movement, a becoming, a journey from what he is to what he is not. This is why all vocations carry the hazard of latent hypocrisy. We are not what we seem. A person who is "called" to a life is more likely to be despised and hated than one who merely does a job. The faithless priest, the avaricious physician, the corrupt judge gather more odium than those who are faithless, avaricious, or corrupt in more pedestrian pursuits.

Nowadays we are all too well aware of our imperfections to imagine that the Christian life is somehow a higher moral calling than that of other people. We take pride in the fact that we consider ourselves no different from other people. We are right to reject any differences based on moral superiority, but we are wrong to conclude that there are no other differences. Christians are different insofar as they live within the realm of Christ. The difference is not so much moral as ontological; that is, Christian faith affects the very roots of our being. We are quite used to our own ordinariness; we have become proud of it. We would not dream of being different from other people. But we are.

Here we come to an apparent contradiction. In the previous chapter we saw that an acceptance of human solidarity was essential for a humble approach to the pilgrimage. Now I seem to be emphasizing the differences. How can this be? Christians are just like everybody else, only more so! It is only when the unity underlying humanity is acknowledged that true and glorious differences can appear. Without that acknowledgment spurious differences based on race, class, sex, and money appear. These are the malicious differences which undermine relationships and destroy the human spirit. To stand as a witness to both human solidarity *and* to each person's unique individuality can turn out to be dangerous. This is where we have to stand. Christians are a people *called* by God, and all vocations arouse hatred.

We might do well to do a bit of hating (after we have finished hating ourselves). It does clear the air. Let us even hate God, the enemy within us, the disturber of our peace. "Hatred of God may bring the soul to God," says Yeats. Hatred of the corruption and wickedness in our deified institutions may bring about their transformation. Hatred of the self-righteous political left or right may herald reform. Hatred of the chaotic unstructured quality of our lives, which the naïve among us call freedom, may usher in new ways of being human. The process of hating in this way can have a renewing and cleansing effect and release those energies needed for the traveler. Unless, like the God in Jung's dream, we have fouled the thing we hold most precious, we scarcely know its value or worth.

Hatred of religion is very important in the religious quest itself. Religion is that which binds up, binds together, in one great whole. In our passion for wholeness it is easy for our man-made religions to "bind up" the wrong things. Religion is a double-headed beast, and has inspired men to the greatest glory and the greatest depravity. It easily parodies its own ideal.

An artist like Ingmar Bergman bears witness to the binding power of religion in his compelling films. He is an artist who found it necessary to eradicate what he believed to be the religious aspect of his life. The religion he had grown up with was a steel trap which bit into his frail being with the terrible teeth of idealism. When he gave up religion he lost his fear of failure. The loss was liberating.

Bergman belongs to the school of those artists (Jung, Hesse, Dürrenmatt) who have rejected the religion of the angry father, the belief in the supreme being who will be placated only by an excellence unreachable by mere mortals. What Bergman and Sartre did was to abandon religion as morality and experience it as gift, as grace. Many a self-styled atheist has abandoned religion because it laid down heavy moralistic burdens on his soul. Most of us still confuse Christianity with morality and cannot discern it as Gospel, Good News. It is only after the experience of Gospel, grace, Good News that implications for behavior can be discerned. Then, and only then, can we talk of morality. Our religion is still in the toilet-training stage, infantile and silly, worrying and fussing over our excrement, over those things which make us unworthy. We are wise, of course, to stay in the infantile state. Everything is well-ordered; the dualism is kept in check. We know where we are. In the Church (as many see it) thinking is not required. In fact, it is a positive hindrance. "Don't worry about the truth, just give them the Catholic faith." used to be the jibe.

At this point on our journey, we must be careful. Having let in the questioning, the all-seeing monster, we must not stop at navel-gazing and remain in a torpor of inactivity. Mesmerized by the demons we have let loose from our particular Pandora's box, we forget there is a final thing to be released: hope. (Pandora, the all-gifted, was the first woman, the Eve, of classical tradition.) Hope is an important final ingredient. It is not a naïve, wishful thinking but rather a sign that there is always more to come. Too many of us suffer from hesitation, from "too much dwelling on the event," from Hamlet's disease. The questioning has an adventurous quality about it if we really take it seriously. It will lead us from our navel into the presence of the transcendent God. Monotheism, claimed Nietzsche in a flash of insight, is "the most monstrous of all human errors." Why? Man's real freedom lay in polytheism. There, in that arena, man at least had a free hand and could play one god off against another. With monotheism we do not stand a chance. It is the wound of transcendence, the wound of an ever-expanding horizon which drives us beyond ourselves, our womb, our mother, our infantile state. We have an indefatigable hunger for reality. We will not rest until we have found it. We will risk madness and death for it. It may be that the future will contain realities impossible for us to bear because of our limited spiritual and moral reserves. Alas, doors once opened are not easily shut. Indeed the flinging open of doors to that ever-expanding horizon is the true merit of humanity. We cannot help ourselves. Perhaps we should try to slam the door in case there is still time?

In terms of the Christian journey there is a joyful sacrament, the celebration of which opens doors to the new. It is the sacrament of *metanoia,* of repentance, of reconciliation. In it we are invited to turn to God, who is the *all,* beside whom we are as nothing. This sounds like the beginnings of a pattern of self-rejection. Not so! Our turning, our conversion away from the pettiness, the sin, the excrement, is a way of affirming that these are lesser realities than the supreme reality of God. Even the sense of our own unworthiness has to be given up. Ironically, it is often our self-rejection which is the hardest of all to surrender. By a peculiar twist the "I" can become proud of being nothing.

There is a story told of a rabbi on the Day of Atonement, beating his breast and uttering the ritual words: "O, Lord, I am *nothing.*" The cantor takes up the refrain: "O, Lord, I am *nothing.*" At the back of the synagogue the janitor decides to join in the lament: "O, Lord, I am *nothing.*" At this the rabbi turns in consternation, pointing to the janitor, and says to the cantor: "Look at him who thinks he's nothing!"

Our nothingness before God is not one of self-rejection and self-recrimination. It is of a different order. It is an emptiness of being springing from adoration. Our emptiness, our nothingness, is that which only God can fill since we have a capacity for the infinite, the transcendent. There is an otherness which we carry within us. The prayer of the publican is a perfect Christian prayer: *Kyrie eleison* (Lord, have mercy). There, in a single utterance, is both praise and sorrow. It is the cry of an emptiness which can be filled only by the love of God. Cardinal Bèrulle, the French mystic of the seventeenth century, put it this way: a human being is "a nothing who is at home with God, whose natural habitat is God, who is capable of receiving God and of being filled by him."

Our nothingness before God is far from negative since it is a nothingness which is God-shaped. This perception of ourselves before God as nothing is wonderfully liberating because we are not permitted even to think of ourselves as bad, guilty, or defiled. To put it more positively, we are to dwell on the marvellous fact *that* we are, not on *what* we are. Our very existence is cause for wonder. As we ponder on this we shall indeed weep because of the many ways in which we squander the gift of our being. We shall also laugh when we see that in spite of everything we are loved, known, and accepted. Divine parents do not, after all, have to be appeased. Our unworthiness, our self-rejection, our sense of defilement, is burned away by the love of God.

We have, however, a long way to go on our journey before the truth of our freedom, in love, is made manifest. We still live in this world with all its demands and pressures; pressures to conform, to toe the line, to produce. In Ionesco's absurd play, *The Future is in Eggs,* a young couple, Roberta and Jacques, are told by their relatives to *produce.* So Roberta lays an egg and, much to everyone's surprise, so does Jacques. The proud parents come in to show off their eggs. "They're my daughter's very first eggs. They look just like her!" exclaim the grandparents. "What are we going to make with these offspring? Omelettes, sausage meat, humanitarians . . . radishes, radicals." What are we going to make of ourselves now that we have begun the journey?

Are we able as Christians, as Americans, as men, as women, to pass through the imitative infantile state? Are we free enough not to be a Xerox copy of the norm dictated by our group? Are we able to transcend our narrowness of vision, our parochialism? Are we able to stop looking to others in our demanding, cannibalistic way, insisting that they lay the particular eggs we like? To be modern, "with it," please lay my eggs, marked "radical" or "conservative" for this or that particular cause.

It is tragic to reflect on what we do with and to one another in this infantile state. But how much worse is a religious infantile state. The imprint of excrement represents the realm of the forbidden, with all that disfigures, spoils, and defiles. It is also an encounter with sin and evil, and, what is worse, with the possibilities of sin and evil within the self. Much of what passes for religion wishes to keep us in this infantile state. By playing on our sense of unworthiness and guilt, religious and political practitioners seek to enslave men and women. The nothingness, far from being creative, becomes a destructive and demonic power by which we are consumed and tyrannized.

In the secular world we bully, we compete, we coerce. Our drives spring from a sense of both disappointment and self-rejection. We need to compensate for the howling emptiness within, and we seek to devour the world itself and to fill up that terrible nothingness which knows nothing of the one thing that could fill it, the love of God. Ursula Le Guin in her magnificent book, *The Farthest Shore*, tells the story of a magician, Ged, who goes in pursuit of the destructive "other," the shadow he has set loose upon the world. Finally he faces the gaping emptiness within: "You exist, without name, without form. You cannot see the light of day: you cannot see the dark. You sold the green earth and the sun and stars to save yourself. But you have no self. All that which you sold, that is yourself. You have given everything for nothing. And so now you seek to draw the world to you, all that light and life you lost, to fill up your nothingness. But it cannot be filled. Not all the songs of earth, not all the stars of heaven, could fill your emptiness."[9] May the Lord have mercy on us all. Yet there is more. For after birth, mother, and excrement (the defiling void within), there comes the fourth anthropological imprint: sexual differentiation. This can hardly be avoided since we are living in a time of excitement, of confusion, of pseudo- and genuine liberation as far as sexuality is concerned. Let us go on.

7.

The Voyage into Sexuality

Then the Lord God said, "It is not good for the man to be alone. I will provide a partner for him." So God formed out of the ground all the wild animals and all the birds of heaven. He brought them to the man to see what he would call them, and whatever the man called each living creature, that was its name. Thus the man gave names to all cattle, to the birds of heaven, and to every wild animal; but for the man himself no partner had yet been found. And so the Lord God put the man into a trance, and while he slept, he took one of his ribs and closed the flesh over the place. The Lord God then built up the rib, which he had taken out of the man, into a woman. He brought her to the man, and the man said:

> "Now this, at last—
> bone from my bones,
> flesh from my flesh!—
> this shall be called woman,
> for from man was this taken."

That is why a man leaves his father and mother and is united to his wife, and the two become one flesh. Now they were both naked, the man and his wife, but they had no feeling of shame towards one another.

Genesis 2:18–25

On the journey of the inner life things do not occur in strict chronological order. Things overlap. They do not knit together easily. They will not stay still. All the states, all the imprints, coexist simultaneously within each of us. There is a deep need here, at this stage of our journey through the dark wood, to pause. Compassion for others, indeed for ourselves, is necessary. Who or what could possibly rescue us from that contradiction of opposites, the contrarieties, the fallenness of everything? There are the deep forces of a deadening atavistic conservatism at work within us which would keep us just where we are. We know them well. Those very same energies which once sustained us take a different direction and seem bent on our destruction. The forces that once held us safe in the womb (until the pressure toward life became too great) redirect their energies and push us into a dependence on mother and mother substitutes: the Church, the community, the party, "One Nation under God." They would now keep us in the infantile state of fearing dark corners, of seeing the bogey man, of fleeing the hobgoblins and devils that haunt the shadows of our cramped lives. In opposition to those conservative pressures, there are those which push us into the realm of the new and the unfamiliar. We have passed through the three stages: birth, mother, the sense of defilement. The pressure toward the next stage has to be of tremendous force if we are to grow. The fourth imprint, sexual differentiation, informs the mythic, interior life of all human beings.

Here we tread delicately. For, while I would do nothing to avoid this area of the wasteland, I am fearful. We are to enter a place of fantasy and confusion.

Let us see if we can pick our way through the sharp and jagged rocks of this part of the country. We must look at the female as she is degradingly portrayed in classical patriarchal mythologies. These are very important, for these images are burned into our souls. We are branded. The classical picture shows Zeus bearing Athene, not from his loins, but from his brain. It is the woman whose creative energies are lower down, in the loins, in the womb. Man's creative impulse is higher up, in his brain. In classical understanding, creation by the power of the word is a masculine trait.

If man has a womb it is in his head. Placed within this classical context, the Genesis myth of Eve being born out of Adam's side does not come off too badly! From Greek mythology itself (let alone classical philosophy) we discern the seeds of that primal heresy: that spirituality and sexuality are opposed. The harm done to individuals and to communities by this particular aberration cannot be over emphasized.

Such was the male's impulse to free himself from the great mother that he overcompensated for her deep numinous quality and so undervalued woman that she was systematically reduced, cut down in the patriarchal mythologies to child-bearing, home-keeping roles. Her position in the ancient world was but a social expression of these deeply rooted symbols. To be sure, there were sibyls, witches, and prophetesses. These were the very signs which proved that man's fear of woman was justified. They were but the needed proof that the female had such powers at her disposal that she needed to be kept down and confined to a manageable role.

One of the silliest and best known of the classical myths is *The Judgment of Paris,* the occasion of the Trojan War. In it we have a male's view of the role of women. Eris (strife) throws a golden apple into the company of the gods assembled for the marriage of Peleus and Thetis. On the apple (it would have to be an apple) is written: "Let the fair one take it." Soon the three high goddesses, Aphrodite, Hera, and Athene, are in a dispute as to the rightful claimant of the golden fruit. Finally they decide to go for judgment to the king's son, the shepherd Paris, before whom is enacted the first recorded *Kallisteion* (beauty contest). From the masculine point of view the excellence of the female resides in three basic qualities: beauty in the form of Aphrodite; constancy and respect for hearth and home and the marriage bed in the form of Hera; and the ability to inspire excellent males to perform excellent patriar-chal deeds in the form of Athene. Since in this male dream world all the contestants are women, it is natural that the winner cheats! Aphrodite is given the apple not so much for her beauty, but for her promise to Paris to give him Helen.

The result is the Trojan War, after which Homer records the return of the Greeks, who go back to their neglected wives after ten years of war. All the wives (with the grim exception of Clytemnestra) have been keeping the home fires burning.

Women have been doing it ever since—at least until recently. In more modern times the ancient Greek ideal has been expressed as *Kinde, Küche, Kirche!* The three K's could be defended but they are not (to say the least) comprehensive! In part, the female revolt is justified. Male and female roles have stiffened into prisons of the soul.

There are signs, good signs, that women do not have to be confined to the three roles to which men have assigned them: Aphrodite, Hera, Athene. There are other signs, bad signs, that the battle of the sexes is about to enter its most bitter and bloody battle for centuries. The extreme feminist position has no room for the male at all. If she is to be free, *he* must be rejected both sexually and spiritually. Some overemphasize sexual differences, others downgrade them. It is ironic that some who are committed to the myth of androgyny are the ones whose long knives are ready-sharpened for sexual slaughter; ironic because the affirmation of sexual differentiation as unimportant would presumably cause them to sheathe their weapons.

Mythologically, the place where the sexes come together is in marriage, and in the Christian myth the symbol of marriage is particularly important. There are a few signs that marriage, and Christian marriage in particular, is gaining a new vitality in the wasteland where we try to "hang in," "hang out," and "hang up." What value is the image of marriage in our self-understanding? It can provide us with a good analogy for our total development as persons whether we are married or not. The image of marriage can be applied to all human beings because there has to be within each one of us those warring, yet complementary, elements: the masculine and the feminine.

But our dual sexuality, as powerful as it is, is only the symbol of a more robust love: the love of God. To confuse humanity with sexuality is disastrous. The notion that it is better to be Helen for one night than to remain "unfulfilled" leads to a straight-jacketing of our own humanity. We forget that this is only one stage (although an important and glorious one) on our journey. Sexual differentiation is only one of the determining factors on our journey to selfhood, on the road home.

Would a matriarchy be better? Hardly! That would be to succumb to the numinous womb/tomb of the great mother. To find a balance, an equilibrium, in our confusion seems well nigh impossible. Could it not be that, in this area as in all the others, we are firmly within the realm of grace, of sheer gift? Heraclitus talked of the phenomenon of *enantiodromia,* of running the other way. It is the principle by which everything sooner or later tends to go over to its opposite. This is what makes me fearful of the uncritical and naïve liberalism and permissiveness in our culture, our Church, our communities, our private lives. Our very openness may call into being (and indeed is already calling into being) its dreadful opposite. The *Iliad* and the *Odyssey* are the classic examples of Heraclitus' principle. The *Iliad* is the epic, the adventure, the dispersion; the *Odyssey* is the return. America has had two hundred years of adventure. Perhaps it is now time to begin the return?

Even in the more neutral mythologies, sex is fraught with danger. There is the whole cycle of myths in which a divine being is slain and cut up, and the parts buried. The parts, in turn, become plants for food—fertility by means of death. Indeed, sex and death are partners because the sexual organs appeared at the time of the coming of death. Death, in principle, was not present while organisms multiplied by simple cell division. In theory, the amoeba is immortal. When it took two to propagate a species, death entered the world. Humanly speaking, death and sex are the correlates of living in space and time. What would have happened if mankind were able to reproduce and yet be unable to die? Tragedy. And so with the converse. What calamity there would be if there were only death and no means of reproduction!

Does sex have to be this battle ground? Do all men fear the

devouring woman? Do all women fear the imperious male whose word is law? How deep does all this go? In the saga of *Beowulf* the most terrible monster the hero fights is female, the mother of the monster Grendel. "Not surprisingly," writes Monica Furlong,

> the battle takes place deep in the waters of a lake, i.e., the unconscious, and it is a bloody and terrible conflict. . . . Odysseus encounters the devouring woman differently—in the attractive form of the nymph Calypso, who seduces our hero with infantile memories of mother and home.[10]

Myth runs deep in all of us. Those heroes and heroines who try to break out of the cycle of fate, of expectation, are especially to be taken notice of in our day. We are to transcend our sexuality, not by avoiding it but by accepting it and embracing it, going through and beyond. Sexual identity then is important, but it does not, and cannot, exhaust all that we are, all that we can possibly mean. Three couples who tried to break free from convention show us a deeper meaning to things: Heloise and Abelard, Tristan and Iseult, Lancelot and Guinevere. I deliberately chose these three because they need resurrecting and rescuing from a cloying romanticism. These stories say with a startling clarity, not that we can do what we like with impunity, but proclaim that the human mystery goes far deeper than conventional morality. Such stories do not advocate license but rather the impossibility of self-justification. Our longing for wholeness points to depths within us far beyond the reach of "goodness." Our stabs at being nice only point more glaringly to our pathetic attempts at being good. Perhaps the most obvious place where our glaring inadequacy at being good stands out is in our sexual relations.

Our quest for wholeness as individuals has to include the sexual stage, but we must not stop there. Our road of wounding and healing lies open. There is Gospel, gift, grace; the only means by which whatever wholeness we have comes to us. I believe Christians, both male and female, have a vital contribution to make in our confused and confusing world. There are other ways, marvellous ways, of expressing one's sexuality other than confining it to the action of "the two-humped beast." These ways need to be expressed vigorously and joyfully, particularly for the benefit of those who define themselves exclusively in narrow sexual terms and are being slowly strangled by their own genitalia.

There are simple and direct physical gestures of affection. There is the tenderness, the caressing, that can be enjoyed by persons of the same sex without our having to label it homosexual. We reach out to one another in the agony of loneliness, and when we do it is instantly labeled. Such labeling makes us more fearful, so our cities and towns become dotted with separate wells of loneliness, with human beings terrified to reach out and touch one another.

There are many wells of loneliness today, men and women are crying out for intimacy. There is a simple and direct longing in all of us to be held, to be caressed, to be cherished. We find it hopelessly difficult to open ourselves up to a variety of intimacies because we fear that there is only one way open to us. Men and women find it almost impossible to relate to one another except in narrowly sexual terms.

Sexuality is an issue in the Church right now, and is focused in the ordination question. This issue is snarled up with all sorts of complications and needs untangling. How far, for example, is the Church really a patriarchy? Does the male priest really have all that much power? What of those middle-aged, middle-class women who dominate the Church's life? Where do we go from here? Is the Church a ruling matriarchate with a thin veneer of patriarchal polity? My women friends claim this is yet another male-concocted smoke screen! They may be right. Power is sometimes a very subtle animal.

Each one of us, in our own way, has begun to go through the fire which transcends this narrow view of sex. If a Christian has not begun to do so, then he has not yet begun his journey. That journey is basically radical and revolutionary in terms of its understanding of the potentialities of the human spirit. Marriage, however, is a good analogy with regard to our total development as persons. Indeed, there has to be a marriage within each one of us of those often warring elements, the masculine and the feminine. Rosemary Haughton, in her stimulating book, *Tales from Eternity*, has suggested that the need for such a marriage of those elements within us is well documented in those myths and fairy tales which used to be part of every childhood. It is more strictly the world of *faerie* rather than *fairy:* the world of mystery and of numinous powers. The cycle of tales which deals with the adventures of the youngest son, who is often gauche and considered not very bright, is particularly illuminating. Naturally, the gauche youth triumphs in the end, but it takes something outside him to release those powers required to transform him into a hero. In many of the stories concerning the youngest son, that outside help comes in the form of a beautiful princess. Just before the young man was about to attack the dragon, "the princess . . . ran up and kissed him on the forehead. Then the prince swung the dragon up into the clouds, and when it touched the earth again, it broke into a thousand pieces."[11]

This sounds as if the role of the princess is merely that of Athene; that is, to inspire the hero to perform heroic deeds. Here, however, the princess is actually the agent, the enabler. Without her, the prince would have no means by which he could conquer the dragon's power. Men and women need to accept and embrace those so-called feminine and masculine qualities within them in order to be transfigured into persons. It is, of course, sheer idiocy to classify virtues according to gender. Christ displayed those qualities characteristic of the true princess in the fairy tales: a strong sense of purpose, a pragmatic approach to circumstances, a deep conviction of the responsibility for the welfare of another.

The Christian is called upon to play the role of the gauche youth. He is not particularly competent. He is ill-suited for his task. He possesses no secret knowledge. Nevertheless, he is called and he responds to the call of adventure. The Christian pilgrim, as inadequate as he is, does not travel alone. In myth and fairy tale the help he needs often comes in the form of a princess who is the bearer of hidden wisdom. The hero must turn to her if he is to survive. In psychological terms, he must open himself up to the female who lives within him.

Using the images of fairy tales, there is, within each one of us, a gauche youth and a wise princess. There are, as it were, two wills, two centers: ours and God's. These two are meant to be one. An open and fulfilled humanity is a wedding between God and the soul, is a joining together of what were once opposing elements. Christian mysticism abounds in erotic and nuptial imagery with regard to our destiny and destination in God. In the world of the fairy tale, the youth and the princess are destined to be married. In some people, as in some fairy tales, there is a long, painful and stormy courtship; in others, there is scarcely a glimmer that the two elements even exist. In still others, the youngest son has never been introduced to the real princess, though he knows of her existence. How do these complementary elements come together and to what extent does it depend upon a person's acceptance of Gospel, gift, and grace in the realm of the Spirit? Our full humanity, as men and women, is a journey, a movement, a calling. It is a wedding.

We are back to the question of vocation. Vocation implies a call from beyond, from the beyond that is within us all. Vocation, journeying, has an "I can do no other" quality about it and presupposes what Christians call grace. We are called to be pioneers, explorers of all that is human. Our pilgrimage has very little to do with feelings of worthiness or unworthiness. Vocation is like being born.

I did not ask to be born. Neither did I ask to be a priest (far from it). Like birth, it is a gift and I am stuck with it. I have to work out my own salvation with fear and trembling within this context. There is my problem. We minister the gift for an arbitrary given and it is precisely this unalterable givenness against which we fight. We live in an age when the fulfillment of the need of the moment is regarded as an inalienable right. Anything is permissible in the pursuit of what we pretentiously call our destiny. We sever relationships with casual brutality and ignore responsibility with self-righteous protestations. We can do anything under the guise of self-discovery. Popular journalism documents well enough the carnage of men and women abandoning responsibility and fulfilling themselves. So a man leaves his wife because she does not fulfill his needs. A wife abandons her family because she feels trapped and wants to be free.

In spite of all that can be said about human beings in psychological and sexual terms, there remains within us a deep and inexhaustible mystery. In theological terms we affirm that a human being is made after the image of God. It is the mark of divinity which drives us mad and gives us hope. It drives us mad because human life is open and unfinished. It gives us hope because life's openness is openness to God himself. This openness leaves us asking many questions. We have to learn to live with our problems and questions. Indeed we have to *live* the questions (to use Rilke's phrase) and learn to live them as the very things which open us up and enable us to grow. Most of our problems and questions are never resolved during the journey, and the striving for happiness, bliss, or fulfillment as ends in themselves is naïve, unrealistic, and foolish from both a secular and a Christian perspective.

Our freedom is dependent on our willingness to surrender, to give up our hold on our life, a hold that will inevitably have to be given up anyway. Our "dying" becomes the agent of renewal and new life. Once our life has been surrendered, our journey ceases to be a fatalistic *given.* It is transfigured into a liberating gift; and, as we have seen, it is not always easy for us to see the difference between life as a given and life as a gift.

Being faithful today is especially hard. Faithful to what? What is it that calls forth our allegiance as we tread our way through the wasteland of shattered symbols and broken images? We have even traveled beyond the point where to talk about the existence or nonexistence of God has any value or meaning. We do have Christ, and Christ is Lord: *Kurios Christos.* The particularity of Christ is one of the givens with which we have to contend. In reality he is the gift which set us free. Whatever else he is, he is not the Buddha or Krishna. Christ is not a mere avatar, an instance of the divine. For Christians he is determinative. Christians, however, often give the impression that they not only acknowledge Christ, they own him as well. They not only claim to know Christ but to know him exhaustively and exclusively. But he is not *our* Christ in any proprietary sense. We do not *own* God and yet we still behave as if we do. As we have seen, in the last century God was Anglo-Saxon. Until recently, he was considered American. God, however, gets out of hand, and no matter how we try to fashion him according to our own likeness, he continually breaks free. That is the divine genius! Christ is, above all, the pilgrim, *the* pioneer. He is out there ahead of us, beyond and above all that we are, in all that we know of life. He is within our deepest selves. Faith in Christ today is not so much blind as blinding. The light shining from all the coming realities is so intense as to be dazzling. Like Samson, eyeless, we feel we do not see the rays of the sun.

Time appears to be slipping away from us with ever-increasing velocity and we wonder if we can cope with the future. Can we, given our present constitution, bear the glories and the burdens that lie ahead? It takes considerable courage and faith to live meaningfully, to keep human life human. The Christian is committed to a life that is as fully human as possible. There are two bumper stickers displayed on cars in a Texas town. One proclaims: "I've found it!" The other, in reaction, answers back: "I lost it—keep on doubting!" The first wishes to announce the new life given to us in Christ. The second wants to make it absolutely clear that, no matter how deep our faith, no one on this side of the grave has ever quite found it. God (whom Jung would call the Self with a capital S) holds us in being. Doubt is the good by which we are driven to transcend ourselves. Faith in Christ, the truly human, does not obliterate doubt. In the true pilgrim, faith and doubt coexist. The latter drives him on the journey. The former gives him grounds for hope. "To come to a doubt," preached John Donne, "and to a debatement in any religious duty, is the voyce of God in our conscience: Would you know the truth? Doubt and then you will inquire."[12]

8.

The Journey to Our True Image

THE WOUND OF TRANSCENDENCE

We now come to the next step of the way illuminated for us by psychology and anthropology. After womb, mother, excrement, and sexual differentiation, comes the complex pattern of sexual relations in the family and in society. Yet there is still more to come. The birthmark of the image of God is the final imprint, which, although not found in the popular textbooks, is certainly hinted at in the new transpersonal schools of psychology. Jung and Freud have done us an incalculable service in analyzing and describing our drive toward transcendence. In some ways they have delineated the fall of man in a far more rigorous and despairing form than the biblical authors could ever have imagined. What could be more of a sign of a "fallen" state than the fiat of psychological determinism? At the same time depth psychology has opened us up as "mysteries." The rich unfathomable world of the unconscious shows us an ever-expanding reality. In the words of the Christian tradition, we are on a journey from glory to glory. Human beings today, then, are confronted with damnation and glory. Psychology itself is in an exciting state of upheaval. It is beginning to realize its limitations and is not so ready to proclaim norms with regard to psychic and spiritual health. Today we are beset by the heresy that the presence or absence of neurosis is the touchstone of truth. One of the dangers of this approach is that it has very little respect for any sort of attempt at objectivity. We all too easily judge a person's statements in the light of some arbitrary standards of mental hygiene. Mad people can say true things! "Oh, she's neurotic, what she says can't be true." is the sort of statement which bedevils all conversation. We tend to do all in our power to avoid *ideas* and attack people instead.

Is the much publicized, popularized Oedipus complex really universal? There is much controversy over this very point, but the evidence appears to be weighted in favor of the affirmative. What does this mean for those of us who claim to be living in the new age? To be made after the image of God is to be scarred with the wound of transcendence. It means that, while who and what we are have been largely determined by our fifth imprint, the family (the often fatalistic triangle of man, woman, and child), we are, nevertheless, not totally determined by that not-so-holy deterministic trinity.

Psychology can prepare for liberation. It can show us where we have been, how we have been trapped and even deformed by the various steps of the inner journey. In this heavily "psyched" age, this is almost too much to bear. We have knowledge, all right (we know we have never broken the umbilical cord), but it is a knowledge which stultifies and petrifies rather than liberates. We need to know and yet we need liberating from what we know. Liberation, in the end, is a matter of faith. We will not gain liberation by dismissing the insights of depth psychology. We must take them seriously. Only by going through the fire can it be overcome. Repression can have disastrous consequences. We dare not avoid the inferno of the passions without disastrous consequences. They have to be faced or else their smoldering power will eventually flare up to destroy.

And the last enemy to be overcome is the phantom of psychotherapy as an end in itself. Why? Because the heavily psychoanalytical approach to life becomes imprisoning insofar as it gives us knowledge of ourselves without the promise of liberation from ourselves. The words "psychoanalysis" and "psychotherapy" are used rather loosely to cover an enormous range of therapies practiced in our contemporary culture. The good therapist, like the good guru, is always trying to do himself out of business. Therapy is a step toward liberation. When therapy is presented to us as a tool, it is a timely aid to the wounded or lost psyche. When it is presented as a metaphysic, a Gospel, it is demonic. We will only be free when we have dared to walk through the dark wood of the soul. A good therapist is like Dante's Virgil. He can take us so far, but not far enough for our soul's full health. Nor would he wish to believe, to doubt, to love, on our behalf. These we have to do for ourselves. The good therapist can help us be free of some of the tyrannies of environment and upbringing. We are not totally determined by our parents, or the circumstances of our birth.

So we take this final pattern of mother, father, child very seriously. This is the nuclear family into which most, if not all, of us are born. It is from this unasked-for mold that every human being is cast. It is true that each of us is unique. We are not cloned from the single cell of our mother or father. Nevertheless, this basic triangle of man, woman, and child is the theater of our development as human beings. It is the stage on which we act out our first loves and first hates. There, in the family, we first learn to fear and to hope. It is an arena of terror. It is also a place of joy and celebration. None of us escapes its powerful formative influence. To know just how far the imprint of the nuclear family has shaped us, may give us a clue as to the frightful limits of our freedom.

My voyage to America from England at the age of twenty-four did something to crack open my mold. Nevertheless, old things still linger on. My socialist heart and my conservative mind (or is it my conservative heart and my socialist mind?) are part of the inherited mold. My instinct tells me that tennis is for the prosperous middle-class, that skiing is well beyond my horizon. My apparently surviving soul is scarred with other such sillinesses. This is precisely where the insights of depth psychology have helped me. The scars seem pretty well healed. But that is not enough. The way of love, the way of transcendence, battered as we are by all imprints, is the only hope. Indeed, every step of the way brings us nearer to the outskirts of the realm of love. Each imprint, when we see it for what it is, reveals to us more clearly the kingdom of grace, of gift, of Gospel. These are the seeds of hope in our helplessness, the intimation that our journey has a destination. We are not going nowhere.

We are going somewhere, and the clue to that somewhere is found in a final, all-embracing imprint: the *imago Dei*. Man is made in the image of God. He is stamped with divinity and that is the key which releases us from the binding power of all the other imprints. Very simply, the imprint of the divine image means that, no matter what has happened to us as we have followed the pattern of the imprints, the last word has not been spoken about us. We are open and unfinished. To be made in the divine likeness is to be made for love by love, to be marked for eternity. That image which shapes all of us has been marred, and, in the words of the saints, we now roam about aimlessly in "the region of unlikeness." In that region, man betrays his own deepest self as he was meant to be: the likeness of God.

One is reminded of the strange plot of Mozart's *The Magic Flute*. It is the basic story of the journey. Prince Tamino has to pass through various stages, analogous to our imprints, before he can win his heart's desire, the Princess Pamina. The plot has its proper share of evils to overcome: a dragon, a wicked queen, and a malignant moor. The theme is common in fairy stories. The hero has to be "tested" and found "worthy" of the "prize." Tamino goes through water and fire to win his bride. The implication is that true happiness is not a right. It has to be won. These imprints of birth, mother, excrement, sexuality, and community have to be transcended if we are to become persons. It is the process called "individuation," with all the broad implications afforded it by modern psychology. We live in the age of Aquarius, the age of water, of the ocean; an age when new ways of comprehending reality are imprinting themselves on our consciousness. The implications are literally infinite because of the last determinative imprint: the imprint of divinity.

Human beings are pilgrims of the transcendent. We are invited to go beyond what we know of ourselves. The spirit of God continually fools us out of our limitations. We are to be pioneers beyond the womb, beyond mother, beyond infantilism. We are even to transcend sexual identity. It is not that we are to deny our sexuality but to understand that our true identity cannot be comprehended merely in sexual terms. Our identity is hidden, even from ourselves. As we have seen, the doctrine that we are made after the image of God proclaims that a human being is fundamentally a mystery, a free spirit. Our role is to be bearers of the spirit. The creative artist is one who carries within him the wound of transcendence. He is the sign that human beings are more than they think they are.

The actor, for example, has his own rich inner life to draw on in his work. His very profession is the exploration of his own hidden depths. A great actor dares to go on an interior adventure when he studies and performs a role in a play. He allows the past to become part of him, to get under his skin. To do this he has to open himself up. For the poor actor, it is an act of self-exposure. For the great one, it is an act of sacrifice. The Christian is to be an artist like the actor. He is the one willing to open himself up and disclose his own secrets.

The great actor, as every great artist, knows the power of the numinous, that is, the pervasive presence of mystery, the throb of the energy behind the universe. To know this, to know God, involves sacrifice, for it is a double experience which elevates and humiliates (or humbles) simultaneously. The mind of the artist, of the genuinely religious person, oscillates, not between right and wrong but between sense and nonsense. This is the awfulness of pushing beyond morality, convention, and custom, beyond the imprints, and learning to live in the terrible order of freedom. Freedom comes to us as a call, a vocation, to respond as fully as we are able to all that human life offers us. Freedom is a call to responsibility. It is the burden of divinity, the wound of transcendence. To be free is to be like God. We do not suddenly become immoral, but we realize that the pusillanimous categories by which we claim to judge moral issues are hopelessly inadequate.

Living in the order of grace, of Gospel, of gift, is to live within the aura of a presence, that "beyond in our midst," and to know that we do not belong to ourselves. Everything subsists within this presence. The person of faith carries the burden of knowing it. This "beyond in our midst," this mysterious other in our lives is God. There is nothing closer to us than God. He is even closer to us than we are to ourselves, closer to us than we are to the self that we know. We *know* it. That is our glory and our tragedy, because knowledge is good but it is not enough. We not only desire to know, we desperately want to be known. *Gnosis* has its limitations. Insight into our state illuminates the landscape, it shows us where we are in the wasteland. It gives us our bearings in the dark wood. But if we are to move on and be healed, there is one more thing needful. We need to be known. This knowledge of being known we call love; but what is that? All we know is that this part of the exploration leads us to Calvary. Love pushes us beyond mere gnosticism, beyond philosophy, beyond a selfish self-awareness into the word beyond words which is the word of Love. Mere intellectual knowledge is not enough. The devils believe in God and tremble. Lucifer, the prince of devils, is said to be pure intellect and *knows* much. He suffers torment because he refuses to love the One he knows.

Here, then, is the first step on the path to love, to be true to the best that is in us, to cleave with love and faith to the little that we do know. This, too, will involve pain and penitence, for having shifted from a cult of self-awareness, of nursing the ego, into the realm of self-transcendence, of self-questing, we shall be burdened with a deep sense of abandonment, of lostness, and of sin. We do not and cannot feel quite "at home" where we are. We are overcome from time to time with the knowledge that we have not only been unfaithful to conventional morality but, more devastatingly, to our own inner self, our own inmost truth.

This inmost truth is a double hunger to love and to be loved *(amare et amari),* and we will go to any lengths to still for a while those hunger pains. The strange hero Henderson, in Saul Bellow's

Henderson the Rain King, has a gnawing insistent voice within him, driving him: *"I want, I want, I want."* and yet he does not know what he wants. Sex or music can silence the voice for a while but it is not long before the descant is taken up again. What do we want? We want love. But are we prepared for the transforming wonder, the transfiguring terror of the love which called us into being?

The point of the Christian journey is the restoration of the broken image which allows the grace of God to flow into wounded men and women to heal them and to restore in them the true image of the divine. To be like God is to be truly a lover, to be truly human.

How, then, is that image restored? Now that we are on the borders of the realm of love, what further steps must we take? To love means to be prepared to be broken up. The restoration of the divine image in us which is love itself involves the shattering of all other images. As our self-image lies at our feet fragmented and broken, the unique intervenes. Love becomes, at last, a real possibility simply because we have no negotiable assets. Love, under these circumstances, can come to us only as a free gift, and love which does not come in this way is not love at all.

That we are loved freely is the hardest of all things to accept. Self-hate and self-rejection blind us to the love which undergirds our very existence. This is the one constant I find in counseling and in confession: that even the most self-assured, self-satisfied, self-possessed people cannot really believe that they are genuinely loved or that they are even lovable. Love has to be earned. There is no such thing as a free lunch! This makes us insecure. It causes us to turn on one another. In the end the impossibility of earning love makes us hate ourselves.

The genius of the demonic is to make us despair, to make us reject our own humanity by rejecting ourselves and others. The devil holds up a mirror to us which shows us as vile and unworthy worms. We forget that being "worthy" is not the thing that matters in the end. The *only* thing that matters is love. Slowly and painfully we practice the art of loving by admitting the possibility that God could love us. We begin to love by allowing ourselves to be loved, accepting the possibility that God could love us! The unique intervenes. God does love us. We are made after his image and this means there is a fundamental relatedness which exists between God and the human race. This relatedness is the most real thing about us. It is a covenant relationship of love which liberates us from the tyranny of self-rejection, from the prison of our low self-image.

As we have seen, this wonderfully close relationship between God and us exists within a cloud, a mystery, a hiddenness, which prevents the love from being finally defined or understood for purposes of manipulation and control. The relatedness, the love, the conviviality, therefore, is not so much something to strive for or achieve but rather something which already *is.* It has only to be accepted. Love, in human terms, is often based on patterns of negotiation and arbitration. The essential covenant relationship which we have with God, with the world, with one another, and within ourselves is trivialized and diminished by our bargaining procedures and by our chronic inability to be lovers. The imprints are signs of our struggle for power and for control (especially in the realm of sexuality). Intimacy in the end is denied us; friendship grows cold, marriage dies, love withers.

As we wait on the borders of the realm of love, the truth begins to dawn on us. Love depends on a disarming act of self-donation, of self-surrender, of self-sacrifice. Most of the time we opt for the relatedness which is based on sheer force: money, prestige, machismo. This is the way of death. If we would live we must wait for the coming of the Spirit.

9.

Entry into the Realm of the Spirit

For many a petty king ere Arthur came
Ruled in this isle, and ever waging war
Each upon other, wasted all the land:
And still from time to time the heathen host
Swarm'd overseas, and harried what was left.
And so there grew great tracts of wilderness,
Wherein the beast was ever more and more,
But man was less and less, . . .

Tennyson, "Idylls of the King"[13]

"The beast was ever more and more but man was less and less." When silence, wonder, adoration are diminished, so are human beings. We imagine we can get by on love and indeed we can. But love shrivels up and dies in the absence of contemplation and adoration. Love, human love, needs to be transfigured, transcended, if it is to be true to its deepest self. It is by love, freely given and freely accepted, that we are recreated after the image and likeness of God. As the author of *The Cloud of Unknowing* put it: "By love He may be gotten and holden, but by thought of Understanding never." Love "understands" that there is no self-fulfillment except in self-surrender. Many of us, dehydrated as we are, need to recapture the sense of inner realities, of what Tennyson calls that "Strong feeling as to the Reality unseen."

"The reality unseen" has something to do with suffering, with love, and with ultimate destiny. It is the realm of the spirit. It comes to us, as we have seen, in hints, echoes, intuitions, myths, and fables—in these strange and often bizarre vehicles of truth. In the full reading of the great stories handed down to us we find not only romance but betrayal; not only triumph but disillusion and decay.

The parallels with our own spiritual journey are painfully obvious. Psychologically, the pattern seems to be universal. There is no way human beings can be transfigured into persons without going through a period of tests and trials. There is nothing instant or automatic in spiritual development. We also strive after outer realities and miss the inner substance.

One of the most famous versions of our search for meaning is found in Wagner's last opera, *Parsifal* (1882). It is a four-hour extravaganza. Parsifal is the questing knight in search of the Holy Grail, the chalice used by Christ at the Last Supper. There are passages in the music which betray a deep, painful, and glorious longing. Wagner's version of the story is important because it throws light on the dangers of our pilgrimage. Some see in *Parsifal* the embryo of the Aryan brotherhood that would culminate in Hitler. Our quest, too, can easily degenerate and become parochial. We develop a private reality, a narrow vision, which we use to exclude, dominate, even to crush others. Wagner fed the German soul. But what of American pilgrims, our pride and arrogance? What of English, African, Chinese pilgrims? How can we learn humility and compassion if our vision is narrowed by local or national interests?

Other critics see *Parsifal* as Wagner grabbing after meaning at the end of an indulgent and luxurious life. Wagner suffered but he suffered in luxury. Is this opera really the belated and despairing repentance of an elderly lover of pleasure? This is a danger and temptation which confronts religious people. When the earthly fires are spent what have we got to lose by investing in the spiritual realm? Some of us sound like eunuchs preaching chastity to the full-blooded. As our own flesh weakens, and people younger than ourselves seem to be enjoying life more than we are, there is a seductive temptation to view the things of the flesh, the things that pass away, as evil in themselves. This is not the Christian way. The flesh does pass away, but it is always the potent symbol of a deeper and more robust reality. Ours is an unashamedly materialistic religion. The God-Man Jesus enables us to take the flesh and all creation seriously.

Was Wagner's repentance somewhat tardy? Is religion only for those who cannot avoid the gaping mouth of death? *Parsifal* is certainly concerned with redemption, with the coming "home" of the true knight, with the return of the hero. As in all forms of the pilgrimage, there is both trial and reward. Yet Wagner's opera is at best a grasping after an ideal rather than the affirmation of a Gospel. The power of transformation is conceived as something which is self-generating. There is, in the end, no gift, no Gospel, no grace. But how the image haunts us! They still sleep deep within us as we continue our journey. Sometimes we are overcome by the sense that we have failed mysteriously to ask the right question about things and, because of this, the whole world appears out of joint. Our vision lacks focus.

To contemplate, to see with all our being: that is our highest function, our supreme activity. To contemplate means to realize that *everything* is under the aegis of the Holy Spirit. "Without vision the people perish," without true insight the wasteland takes over, primal chaos has free rein. Knowledge of the nature of things means to be native to them. It means having the inner substance of the thing known flowing in our blood. It means an intimacy with what Gerard Manley Hopkins called the "inscape." Our nature is not yet in tune with things as they really are.

For the Christian pilgrim, the mystery of the way things really are lies in contemplation of the Incarnation. To be in Christ is to be in tune with the universe and to be native to the things of God. That is why the Christian tradition defines us in terms of the divine.

When the Christian pilgrim begins to live from a center which is not his flabby unfocused ego, he enters into a new dimension of living which the saints call divine. This is how we can be conscious of ourselves by being Christ-conscious rather than self-conscious.

We imagine that our ignorance will save us, that our failure to perceive will somehow prevent the destructive chaos from breaking in. This peculiar logic governs much of our lives. Even what knowledge and insight we do have into the mystery of things is highly dangerous. King Arthur's unwitting incest with his half sister, Oedipus marrying his mother, Uzzah struck dead for steadying the Ark of God: all these were sins of ignorance which had to be paid for. Deeply religious people (in the best sense) are always in great danger of using what light they have for their own self-preservation. By grasping after holy things for our own use and self-preservation we invite disaster. It is thus that we wound ourselves.

So it is with our religion. Faith should be a protective garment for the pilgrimage. Instead, it becomes a superficial cloak to protect us from those very realities within which we claim to be living. Small doses of Christianity serve as an inoculation against the real thing. Sunday by Sunday people preserve themselves from an attack of serious Christianity by taking in a small amount. Like smallpox, Christianity is best avoided by a minor injection of the disease, of that incurable God-sickness (to use Karl Barth's phrase). We, too, turn the most sacred mysteries into a blanket of self-preservation, and with frightening consequences. The result is a paralyzing shallowness in religion which parodies, mocks, the real thing. That is why a man like Kierkegaard raged vehemently against much that he saw in Christianity as an established religion. It had the outward forms without the inner substance. It lacked the passion and vitality to transfigure human life. The only way through is by self-surrender in a life punctuated by stillness and contemplation. We must be still.

It is hard to wait. We cannot endure the sense of emptiness that comes over us when we sit still. One of our problems is that very few of us have developed any distinctive personal life. Everything about us seems secondhand, even our emotions. In many cases, we have to rely on secondhand information in order to function. I accept the word of a physician, a scientist, a farmer, on trust. I do not like to do this. I have to because they possess vital knowledge for living of which I am ignorant. Secondhand information concerning the state of my kidneys, the effects of cholesterol, and the raising of chickens, I can live with. But when it comes to questions of meaning, purpose, and death, secondhand information will not do. I cannot survive on a secondhand faith in a secondhand God. There has to be a personal word, a unique confrontation, if I am to come alive.

There are many "peddlers of meaning" who will readily tell us what we *mean*. The churches at their worst have been and are traffickers in secondhand meaning. It is true that there are many aids, guides, and maps to help us, but in the end, we have to allow meaning to penetrate us. No one can believe, hope, and love in our place. We must do these things ourselves. Such things have to come to us directly, firsthand. The only kind of knowledge that matters, in this regard at least, is experimental knowledge: that is, a glimpse of what happens to us and in us from moment to moment, of what is happening right now.

It is as if we have within us a form of radar, a mechanism by which we reach out and come into contact with the realities around us. We can, of course, get by without reaching out much at all. We develop the habit of not doing so and we become numb and insensitive. In fact, slowly and imperceptibly we begin to die. We rot from within, we fade, we wither.

There is one simple exercise we could do each day to use our radar. It is so simple that one might be tempted to ignore it. Sit comfortably (not too comfortably) in a chair with your eyes closed and breathe quietly and evenly for a few minutes. Then listen. You will hear odd sounds, a bird call, the hum of distant traffic, a child playing. There is, if we would listen, a whole symphony of sound. In fact we are programmed to tune out rather than tune in to all that the world offers eye and ear. If we really listened we would hear "the roar on the other side of silence." There are many books available today giving detailed information concerning techniques of stillness, of listening, of seeing. Christians do not go into the desert place of the heart on an empty stomach. The empty space within, as we have seen, can be a place of madness and of terror without the protection of an interpretive framework provided by a myth or a story. The Bible contains the story of the Christian journey. The Eucharist is its heart presented in dramatic form. Both provide sustenance for the desert experience. They give focus to "the immense meaning" which surrounds us. A balanced Christian diet has always been regular Bible reading, the sharing in the common meal of the Eucharist, and the daily practice of interior prayer. It is as simple and as difficult as that.

Meanwhile we have stumbled into or deliberately entered the desert to contemplate—that is, to see and to listen. Let us sit upon the ground, just as we are, wherever we are, in a rich and baffling environment of womb, mother, infant, sex, family. We may feel a little battered: chastened but not killed! Now we are to *look,* listen. We prepare for the coming of the spirit of love by entering as far as we can into that spiritless state which is called Nirvana. Nirvana: it suggests the end of our pain, the end of our exploring. We have ceased to search for home because there is no home. There is only Nirvana. This concept, central to Buddhist and Hindu thought, suggests a state of painless oblivion. It goes hand in hand with another idea, which regards the world of our senses as Maya, illusion. Many of us in the West have embraced these two ideas uncritically. We have rightly perceived that much of the so-called enlightenment of the West is based on idolatry; that is, on giving our ultimate allegiance to penultimate things. Our way, however, lies not in withdrawal from the things of the senses but in their transfiguration and redemption.

The concept of Nirvana can be helpful to us if we remember that human emptiness has the correlative of divine fullness. In the Hebrew tradition, the prophets knew that the austere otherness of God, the I AM, was but the other side of his equally awesome nearness. Nirvana, which speaks of annihilation and emptiness, also has its correlate.

But no word coming from the so-called mystic and inscrutable East has been more misunderstood than Nirvana. The analogy is given of the surface of a pond blown by the wind. When the wind (or in this case the friendly energy of an Irish Setter) disturbs the surface of our pond in Connecticut, the image of things is broken and disturbed. Everything is fragmentary and continually flickering. If I am patient, the wind stops, and the surface becomes smooth and still: *Nir,* (beyond or without) *vana* (the wind.) What happens when the wind stops? I look and I *see,* not the broken images but the perfectly formed reflection of the whole sky, the trees and shrubs along the edge of the pond. But that is only a part of what I see. If I look further, I see beneath the water itself. I peer into its quiet depth. The plants, the darting fish, the tadpoles, the lovely stony bottom. Nirvana. As we learn to be still, we begin to see, we begin to heal. Ordinary things, everyday activities, take on a new quality. The dark wood becomes less menacing, or, to change the image, the wasteland gives way to a less dry and rocky prospect. Flowers do bloom in the desert. This is the promise of Isaiah: "Let the wilderness and the thirsty land be glad, let the desert rejoice and burst into flower" (Isaiah 35.1).

This is what is meant by contemplation. Contemplation is seeing and living in the spirit of what we have perceived. All Christian discipline is designed to sharpen our perception, to harness all those energies of loving, vibrant yet disconnected, within us. This kind of seeing is the herald of true freedom. The art of contemplation is deemed necessary by all the great religions if one is to press forward as a pilgrim. Contemplation is also a cleansing activity since spirituality is not immune to corruption and defilement. It is a breakthrough beyond the mere appearance of things. So, to paraphrase Blake, the wise man and the fool do not *see* the same tree. Contemplation, the art of seeing, involves the shock of revelation, the shock of catching a glimpse of things as they really are.

The Japanese tea ceremony, for example, is a brilliant and artistic exercise in perception. What could be more ordinary than drinking tea with a few friends? It was only when I experienced a

Western effort to share in the ceremony that I began to appreciate its delicacy. What really happens when you begin to pay close attention to detail: the beautiful simplicity of the teahouse, the careful selection and arrangement of the flowers, the beauty of the cups themselves, the graceful art of conversation, the meticulous choice of guests. It is not an overstatement when it is said that the mastery of tea is the entry into freedom. What a strange reversal from our Western assumption. It is structure which enables a thing to be free. Chaos means bondage. With us, the reverse is true. The noise and confusion of the American cocktail lounge is ugliness and chaos. A bottle of wine shared with a few friends may have something of the pattern of the Japanese tea ceremony.

This close attention, this being totally present to the situation, can be applied to all that we do. The Japanese have grasped the delicate relationship between structure and freedom. They know instinctively that formality and liberty go hand in hand, that playfulness and duty, far from being opposites, are complements. There is the play language of polite Japanese conversation. You do not, for example, arrive at Tokyo, you *play* arrival at Tokyo. The German word *Pflecht* (duty) is related etymologically to the English words *play* and *pledge*. What a liberty and joy is released in us when we can see duty related to playfulness! Is it possible for us to see and even to live such a connection? Nirvana! Can we see? Dare we see?

What I see when I sit by our pond is not all beautiful. A dead fish floats silently on the pool's still surface. It smells. There is death. Only by being still do we *see*, perhaps for the first time. It is glory and pain. My child sitting by my side suddenly sees the lifeless corpse of the floating fish for what it is, and is filled with dread. Nirvana.

Nirvana is "beyond or without the wind." What a contrast to the wind, the creative wind of God passing over the void at the dawn of creation! Nirvana, stillness, prepares us for the penetrating whirlwind of God's love. It is Nirvana which helps us transcend the imprints (experienced, alas, as deterministic blueprints) and overthrow their tyrannical power. Contemplation pushes us into the realm of freedom, the kingdom of God, the place of grace, gift, and Gospel. Prayer begins in us the restoration of the divine image, in all its hiddenness and wonder. It brings us closer to "the region of likeness" and every prayer is an act of letting the old self go. It involves a "dying." The grain of wheat falls into the ground and dies. Dead, it is destined to bear much fruit.

Poor Alice in *Through the Looking Glass* has to run furiously in order to stay in the same place. We, on the other hand, have to learn to stand still in order to continue our journey. We must stand still. We must learn to *be.* The more we run around, the more we lose touch with ourselves, the less of us there is. The creative center is switched off. We cannot keep uprooting ourselves and expect to remain whole. The still journey of the soul takes forever. After I have been through a very busy period, I feel all strung out, distended. In fact, there is very little that I can identify as *me.* It takes much more time than I am usually prepared to give for all those bits and pieces I call *me* to get back together again. For me, the summer is usually the time when my fragments come back together after a year of movement and talk. I wait. Nirvana. I try to wait in a desert place and watch. As I write now I can see the beauty of the desert and the mountains of northern New Mexico—simple beauty.

There is only one appropriate and adequate response: adoration and thankfulness. Waiting in the desert is an act of love. This waiting is a kind of creative dying which the soul has to bear. There is a Latin inscription on an anonymous early Christian grave: *Dum vivimus moriendum est, ne moriamur quando morimur:* we must die while we live lest when we come to die we shall be dead indeed. But how do we do this?

The imprints on the psyche all point to the fact that we are born too soon. We have to accomplish outside the womb what other animals are able to do comfortably and safely inside. It is reckoned that a human being *qua* animal needs another twelve months in the womb to complete the necessary growth: twenty-one months all told. Our lack of hair is a fetal trait, and our numerous psychological difficulties are functions of the prematurity of our birth. We should not be surprised to find ourselves *das kranke Tier* (the sick animal) of Nietzsche. A human being, at times, seems little more than a decadent ape. So our birth and the impulse toward rebirth does not wait until we are ready. Just as we are thrust out into the world twelve months too soon, so the pressure of the spirit pushes us beyond the imprints of nature, whether or not we feel ready or worthy. Bits and pieces of what we call ourselves are left all over the place, disjointed, distended. There is barely enough of us left to enjoy what we call life. We wander around looking for a place where all those separated pieces (and new pieces yet unborn) can come together again. We are born with an ache for transcendence.

We know that there is within us a deeper mystery than the cookie mold of birth, mother, infantilism, sexual identity, and family pressure. Life cannot be reduced simply to the categories of neuroses and complexes. The Oedipus complex may be universal but is that *all* there is? Can I really be reduced to my sexual preferences? Is there little more to me than a heap of hormones? We need to contemplate, to be still, in order to see that there are movements and pressures within us: mysteries. We *know* that we bear the divine image.

To know that there is an abyss, a mystery within us, is no comfort to us, at least not at first. There comes with this kind of knowledge an implicit invitation to explore and we already know that the first part of the journey involves our passage through the desert, through the place of thirst, of emptiness, of fantasy. The pattern of these encounters is given us at our birth. Does not all this sound pessimistic, fatalistic? It does, and would lead to despair were it not for the fact that beyond the prescribed pattern there is that which is freeing and glorious. The imprints then are the threshold of mystery, its outer limits, the edge of an inexhaustible universe. When we talk about the inner life this is what we mean: the exploration of this inner and outer inexhaustible universe. It is neither ascetical gymnastics nor a jellylike passivity. As we have seen, it is the desert place, the formless void, which we discover at the heart of the human consciousness. It is the gateway to the realm of the spirit. It is Nirvana: stillness to see and feel the coming of the wind of the spirit which thrusts us into the world of action. It is the stillness which provides *meaning* for those actions we are prompted to take. It was the Holy Spirit that moved over the still waters of the deep and blew up a creative storm. Stillness, silence were waiting for the creative fiat and we are to echo that rhythm of stillness and creativity.

Exhausted from our journey through wood and wasteland, let us rest and do nothing, not that nothing may be done, but that the spirit which moved once may move again. Nirvana prepares us for the spirit:

> In the beginning of creation, when God made heaven and earth, the earth was without form and void, with darkness over the face of the abyss, and a mighty wind that swept over the surface of the waters. God said, "Let there be light," and there was light; and God saw that the light was good, and he separated light from darkness. He called the light day, and the darkness night
>
> (Gen. 1:1–5).

10.

The Beginning
of Transfiguration

The Lord God took the man and put him in the garden of
Eden to till it and care for it. He told the man, "You may
eat from every tree in the garden, but not from the tree of
the knowledge of good and evil; for on the day that you eat
from it, you will certainly die." Then the Lord God said, "It
is not good for the man to be alone. I will provide a partner
for him." So God formed out of the ground all the wild
animals and all the birds of heaven. He brought them to the
man to see what he would call them, and whatever the man
called each living creature, that was its name.

Genesis 2:15–19

When all things began, the Word already was. The Word
dwelt with God, and what God was, the Word was. The
Word, then, was with God at the beginning, and through
him all things came to be; no single thing was created
without him. All that came to be was alive with his life, and
that life was the light of men. The light shines on in the
dark, and the darkness has never mastered it.

John 1:1–5

We have reached the realm of the spirit where things are called
by their proper name. Here there is no crisis of identity. There is
a name and a place for everyone and everything. God calls us out
of our nothingness, our emptiness, and invites us to be someone.

He *names* us and we are destined to share in the creative work of the word of God by giving things their true names. How do we do this? We contemplate them, we see them in all their glory by the power of the spirit. Our emptiness has been filled, the void within opened to infinity. The spirit of the Lord, united with our spirit, fills the whole world.

The power of the spirit is manifest in the naming of things. Calling things by their proper names is a dangerous art and the misnaming of things is a great and terrible evil. Naming is the means by which human beings structure their reality. It can be a way of bending and twisting it destructively. Naming has to do with identity. It is a creative or demonic art which conveys being and identity on the thing named. Name-calling is a method of robbing others of their identity and of diminishing and impoverishing their person.

The power of the spirit in the naming of things is beautifully expressed in Ursula Le Guin's story of magic and one magician's search for his true self. In *A Wizard of Earthsea* the apprentice magician has to learn the true names of things. He must be able to distinguish reality from appearances. In one scene, the novice, named Ged, is moved to wonder as the magician, called the Master Hand, changes a small pebble into a glittering jewel. The master warns the novice:

> But you must not change one thing, one pebble, one grain of sand, until you know what good or evil will follow on the act. ... A wizard's power ... is dangerous. ... It is most perilous. It must follow knowledge, and serve need. To light a candle is to cast a shadow. . . .[14]

Naming in myth and fairy story has always been associated with power and identity. Thus, Adam *named* the beasts; in the *name* of the Father, the Son and the Holy Ghost; let his *name* not be remembered; thou shalt not take the *name* of the Lord thy God in vain; and so on. The process by which we name things and by which we are named is one which gives life its focus and meaning. Our spiritual journey is undertaken in order that we may discover our real name, that is, our true identity. Only God knows our real name, who we really are. We are on the voyage to that discovery.

Naming is the clue to such identity and purpose as we have. It is also the source of inner power. In the famous fairy tale, as soon as the princess had guessed the true name of the dwarf, Rumpelstiltskin, his power over her was destroyed. It can, of course, be taken to mean too much. The fact that my name is Alan has very little to do with my identity and sense of purpose (although I suspect it has more to do with it than I know; from Alan Watts I have learned that "Alan" means "hound" and "harmony.") When a total stranger calls me Alan, the name is virtually meaningless. When my wife calls me Alan, name and identity are very close. When God calls me by name, then and only then, is Alan my real name. Insofar as we seek to utter the word beyond words, our life has at least some limited meaning. It coheres after a fashion. It makes some sort of sense. Without it we would not survive. For some of the time we all have to make do with limited meanings and approximations with regard to coherence and sense.

On the journey with God and to God in the power of the Spirit, we slowly increase our capacity for bearing reality, for bearing glory. In this way we see, with the professor in Tom Stoppard's play *Jumpers,* that "atheism is the crutch for those who cannot bear the reality of God." Belief in God entails fearful risks. For in him we find our true identity. By him we are known by *name.* As we begin to know who we are, so also the final and eternal imprint of the *imago Dei* takes hold upon us and fills us with a new spirit even as we are called by name.

In principio erat verbum; En arche en ho logos; In principle, at the root of everything, basically, there is the creative Word, mystery. Theology, as Paul Tillich pointed out long ago, is taking rational trouble *(logos)* about a mystery *(theos).* What then is this word? What is it that lies at the heart of being? In Judaism it is the divine name. It is the Tao that cannot be spoken, the Brahman of

Hinduism, the Ungrund of Jacob Boehme, the Eternal Thou of Martin Buber. For Bonhoeffer it was "the man for others," and this "man for others" was Bonhoeffer's answer to the question "Who is God?" The true name of God cannot be spoken. Moses asked God his name. "I am that I am" (Ex 3:14) was the reply. The Christian God will not be named, will not be manipulated. Because we are made after the image of the unnameable God no one can finally and irrevocably name us. Our real name is beyond the reach of manipulation and control. Whenever we name our god, we can be sure that we worship an idol. *Si comprehendis non est Deus* is the great principle of Augustine: if you think you have understood, it is not God.

For the Christian, *theos* (mystery) resides in the concrete historical revelation of the unity of the whole human race with that mystery *(Christos),* which in turn is inseparably tied to the person of Jesus. He is God's word to us in time and space, in whom is revealed the secret of our true identity.

The power of the word, of naming, is not, of course, confined to Christianity or to Judaism. It is present in all religions and the evidence from anthropology points to the fact that it is universal. The names of things, it seems, are intrinsic, and our poverty with regard to meaning is directly related to the impoverishment of language.

In the *Kabbalah* even the sounds and forms of the letters of the alphabet are regarded as the very elements which constitute reality. Aleph, Beth, Gimmel, Daleth: they contain all the mysteries of the entire universe. It was believed that the Hebrew language itself was the means by which the inwardness of the divine name was revealed.

The title *Baal Shem* (Master of Name) was given to those who knew the true name of beings and things. It is given only to those who live intimately within the secret of the universe. The task of the Baal Shem is to bring the names of people and things closer to the name and, in this way, to be a means by which all things are united to God. The correct pronunciation of names is very important. Because the sound of the name shapes the reality, we have a strange attitude toward the names of our friends and acquaintances. "His name is Algernon but he doesn't *look* like an Algernon; he looks more like a Fred."

In the Tantric tradition, Sanskrit is a holy language and the correct pronounciation of the name of any god will cause him to appear. The name is the audible form of the god. The supreme word, of which the whole universe, visible and invisible, is a manifestation, is the *logos*. In the Indian tradition it is the mystic syllable *aum* or *om*. Just as that single syllable *om* is a verbal manifestation of the whole universe, so my name is a verbal revelation of my own inner self and a source of great spiritual strength.

All naming, all language has this mysterious quality. When we perceive the word in its true form we realize that we are in the presence of the holy. Words have a power and life of their own and we are always saying more than we know. The Freudian interpretation of *Little Red Riding Hood* as a sexual morality story is legitimate, if a little hair-raising. The danger is to limit such things to *one* interpretation, one naming. Everything Freud sees is there, but that is *all* he sees. There are many, many levels. The art is to see the deep interconnectedness of things, and not reduce them to a narrow, one-dimensional level.

What, for example, is the inner reality of *Hansel and Gretel?* Those two names, on a superficial level, conjure up the fairy story set to Humperdinck's delightful music. But there is more to these names than meets the eye. *Hansel and Gretel* expresses one of the deepest fears within all of us (particularly as children): namely, the fear of being eaten. "I could eat you up!" we say to a pretty child. The witch who lives in the gingerbread house is another manifestation of, say the Hindu Mother, the goddess Kali, who is represented with a long tongue to lick up the lives and blood of her children. Within the mind of the child there is fear of his whole universe being torn apart. For the death of the mother involves a death of the self. All this and much more is hidden within the names Hansel and Gretel.

Now language itself is being torn apart, or rather, there is a language war going on where sense and meaning are lost in a barrage of words. Watergate bore witness to the incredible damage that has been done to language. ("I then communicated with him telephonically.") We have developed a new jargon devoid of any moral content or spiritual bite. The phrase "at this point in time" has become a joke, the prelude to telling a lie. The Watergate Hearings, the covering of any news item by the mass media, reveal to me something of the reason why communication is so difficult today, why the word has lost much of its power. Watergate is the name of the pervasive corruption that has weakened the country. The name Watergate has changed us irrevocably, placed us at an ultimate crossroad.

George Orwell wrote in *Politics and the English Language,*

> If thought corrupts language, language can also corrupt thought. . . . One ought to recognize that the present political chaos is connected with the decay of language, and that one can probably bring about some improvement by starting at the verbal end.[15]

Saturation and overexposure kills. Every letter written, every conversation entered into, is somehow public property, possible courtroom material. It is as if everything we do or say is taped, monitored, photographed, and filed, and to no good purpose. No wonder we are fearful to reach out, to touch one another, to speak the word; by such things we are implicated in a crime for which there is no name. Kafka's mad and maddening world is already with us. Just as we have gotten rid of the image of St. Peter sitting at an enormous desk by the pearly gates and thumbing the leaves of a gigantic ledger in which is recorded all that we have ever done, we find that the great tome has been thrown out of heaven and is firmly placed on earth. We are on file, recorded, set down.

Does this sound like paranoia, madness? It is. My madness is mixed from the data of our society and the disease of my own soul.

I *am* paranoid about the loss of the word, and above all, the word beyond words, in our time. I am tired of having to wade through a mass of jargon, of "consultants," "task forces," "experts," "advisers," "chairpersons" to find that language has been impoverished in the process. Such words as sin, obedience, salvation, repentance, redemption, transfiguration—glorious words brimming over with significance—are being replaced within the Church by the ersatz vocabulary of the behavioral sciences. Theology cannot be reduced to sociology without drastic truncation, no more than biology can be reduced to the categories of physics and chemistry. "Bishop" does *not* equal "task force coordinator." There are no exact equivalents, there is no neat correspondence between the world of the spirit and the world of General Motors. The analogy breaks down and I burn and bleed and am ashamed to find myself part of that number who have capitulated, who have succumbed, not to the word beyond words but to the word devoid of meaning. There is no fire in the belly, no word from the Lord. "And the word of the Lord was not heard in the land." At the gateway to the land of the spirit we turn and run back into the wasteland. Is there any word that brings *life*, that "makes the god present" today? Piaget tells of a boy of six-and-a-half who said, "If there weren't any words it would be very bad. You couldn't make anything. How could things have been made?"

We look for the word of Life, for focus and identity and meaning, and we find ourselves lost and abandoned in a morass of words without *the* word. There is an intimate relationship between syntax and sense, between grammar and order.

The reason we have taken this pilgrimage through the wasteland, through the labyrinthine world of myth, fantasy, and psychology, and the imprints of psychology, is that it is only by way of pilgrimage that we shall find the revival of language, the revival of meaning, the true pattern of existence which is the salvation of our souls. The endless cycle of human business and activity makes us impervious to language as genuine communication. We are deaf to the word. We understand words, but the word is not allowed to reach us. This is a deadly thing. Mere words do not hear life, they bring death. So we conspire at the death of the word of Life. The Christian hope is that in Christ, death itself becomes a life-giving event. Death and resurrection, the Christian secret itself, is not only a word, but *the* word beyond words, a word which is nothing less than a creative event in the human heart. You and I, thank God, may begin to mean something after all. We are on pilgrimage to some purpose. It is a journey to death, yes, but also a journey to God. The Gospel proclaims that even when we have ceased to believe in God, he never ceases to believe in us.

11.

The Journey Comes Full Circle

BECOMING A CHILD

We have come a long way. The journey has, at moments, been exhausting. The journey into the interior is like going into a maze. The theme of the maze, the labyrinth, the web is common in the literature of mythology. In each case secret knowledge is required if we are to get through. Theseus needed the thread of Ariadne to find his way back through the Cretan labyrinth after he had killed the Minotaur. The idea of this labyrinth is important in our Christian journey. We journey to its center and have to find our way home again through its complex corridors: the end of our exploring is to come home as if to discover it for the first time. Originally the labyrinth itself was an enormous and complicated sarcophagus, a tomb. In the mythologies of ancient Crete and Babylon, the plan of the labyrinth was closely associated with the internal organs of the body. The object of the tomb-builder was to make it as much like the body of the mother as he was able. Death was a return to the womb to await another birth. Theseus' journey to the center of the Cretan labyrinth is a journey of rebirth, a journey we all have to take (perhaps more than once) to be born anew, to reshape images, to reforge words so that they mean something once again.

The image of the labyrinth, the womb/tomb, bears witness to our double hunger to cheat death and be born again, a double yearning for self-surrender and for self-fulfillment. The journey through the maze of this world to which we are so heavily and irrevocably committed holds out the promise of both. If we surrender to its complexity, will it not yield to us its secrets? We will endure the torments and terrors of the way so long as there is a promise of treasure at the end of our journeying.

The theme of the painful journey is taken up superbly by the biblical writers. The Israelites were supremely a people of the journey, the Exodus. They, and the Christians who came after them, were a people of the way. The Torah, the holy law itself, literally means the signpost along the road. So begins the great Psalm 119: "Blessed are those that are undefiled in the way: and walk in the law of the Lord."

Sin is leaving the road, and metanoia, repentance, a return to the highway; and the prophets were forever calling upon the recalcitrant Israelites to come back. Both Judaism and Christianity call upon their adherents to move, to march, to journey. The initiates in both religions know that it first leads into the desert.

Christianity itself was first known as "the way." Indeed, the early Christians thought of Jesus himself as the way. He is the road and the map by which we are guided through the maze. He is the journey and the journey's end. He is the one who rescues us from our inability to move forward, who snatches us out of the jaws of the tiger, the tiger of our despair as we face all the ways open before us and as we are so frozen by moral and spiritual bankruptcy that we are unable to choose which way to go. In mythological terms Christ undoes the work of "the fall," he tears down the signs of No Way, No Exit, that hover over human existence.

The image of the fall is found in many mythologies: images of being trapped, of being prevented from being born, of being continually at "the ninth month;" all these bear witness to our fallen condition. Christ as liberator will rescue us from all that tends to destroy us. Above all, he will liberate us from the pathetic parody we make of Christianity itself. There is a promise of rescue from mythology, psychology, mysticism (the way to God by self-awareness and special incommunicable knowledge). The only true knowledge is love itself and that is not marketable or saleable stuff. It is not born of technique or of expertise. It is always a gift.

Christ is the word to us in the word beyond words, beyond our strivings. This is a *dogma:* this is the way the universe *is.* We should not be afraid of the word dogma. G. K. Chesterton pointed out that there are only two kinds of people: "those who accept dogmas and know it, and those who accept dogmas and don't know it."

The dogma of Christ runs something like this: If you would live, you must follow the way of death and resurrection, not as a work or a spiritual exercise but as an act of love. We can make this act of love only insofar as we know that we are loved. Indeed, we can love only if we are loved. This is the hardest of all dogmas: to believe that we are loved just as we are. It is the most demanding of all Christian doctrines: to accept that we are accepted.

The Christian life is one of sacrificial love. At the heart of our story is a tree, or rather two trees; one of Adam and the other of the new Adam, Christ. The cross is the tree under which Adam is buried. Both trees are double-sided. They are bearers of life *and* death. In other mythologies too, there is a double-sided tree; one side green and alive, the other side dead and dry. There comes a time when "it is the dry branches and not the green, of the universal tree around which the heavens spin, that must be grasped and painfully climbed."[16] It is the same tree but there are moments on the journey when our climbing has to be on the dry and dead side. So also with the dreadful and yet life-giving mother-goddess Kali: the blood from her left side brought death, and that from her right side, life.

We experience the same coexistence of life and death as members of the Church. As we progress along the way we discover that not only are we, as individuals, made in the likeness of God, but so is the human race. As such, no one can do without a church, for individual restoration rests upon corporate restoration.

My destiny is bound up with yours. As we journey on we discover that your story, as unique as it is, is also my story. We find, together, that we are not so much to "do our own thing" as to discover "God's thing" for us. Politically and socially we fluctuate between a chronic individualism on the one hand and a fearsome all-embracing totalitarianism on the other. The Christian doctrine of catholicity tries to do justice to our individual and collective nature. We rightly fear the twin dangers of isolation and absorption. In the Orthodox Church the word for catholicity is *sobornost*. Catholicity has a legal ring about it; sobornost suggests a marvelous, free, and freeing coherence of the human race in love.

The more I travel, the more I am overcome with the sense that I *am* what my brother is. If he is fallen and depraved, then so am I. If he is glorious and dazzling, so am I. I have often wrestled with the question, "Can one 'leave the Church' and still be a Christian?" I have always, until now, come to the conclusion that one cannot be a Christian outside the Church, simply because to be a Christian involves commitment to community. *Now* I would give a slightly different answer. The Christian life is a continual process of leaving the Church as institution, as trapped by either tradition or modernism, as that which does our praying, thinking, and even loving for us—yes, the Church as Mother. But the Christian way is also a continued rediscovering of the Church as a community in which it is possible for persons to be freed and healed. I can blame the Church as institution for so much, and much of the time I am, in all honesty, quite justified. It is easy to forget that when my friend touches me, when the broken bread ministers to my brokenness, there *is* the Church in action. At first, I took my discontent with the Church, my terror at the possibility of meaninglessness, and the burden of God's silence as the growing evidence that, in fact, I was an atheist. But this kind of atheism seems to me peculiarly salutary in that it washes away the flotsam and jetsam of all those fabricated images of what I called my God. Hatred of God *can* bring the soul to God and even into the Church. This hatred burned in Martin Luther before his heart was inflamed with the conviction of salvation by faith alone. "I did not love, yes, I hated the righteous God who punishes sinners, and secretly, if not blasphemously, certainly murmuring greatly, I was angry with God." Raging at God and at the universe is common among those of us who recite the psalms daily. I rage at God for the *isness* of things. I am angry that I was not "in on" the planning stage of my own life! I rage at the fact that all the journey has done is to bring me back to childhood.

This ambivalence, or rather growth, in our attitude to God and the Church is expressed by Nietzsche in *Thus Spake Zarathustra*. There he describes three metamorphoses of the spirit in the form of the camel, the lion and the child. Our first impulse as newly professed Christians is to be like the camel and to bear as much of the world's ills as possible. Oh, to be useful, or needed! Eager to bear much, we kneel down like a camel in order to be well-loaded. And in the same way that the burdened camel speeds into the desert, so we, carrying the burdens of the world, rush headlong into the unknown. After the first flush of enthusiasm we begin to realize that we have been cheated. The young man or woman discovers that he or she is not, after all, going to save the world. The newly ordained priest soon discovers that he, too, has his limitations. The monk or nun finds that the religious life is far from his or her expectations. Community is defined by one of the Sufi masters as "Irrationals unified by hope of the impossible." To many of us who struggle to live the Christian communal life, this seems apt. There grows within us all an insidious resentment because we thought we had played it all by the rules. We were, for the most part, submissive. We bent our backs eager for the burden, desperate for something to *do*. We did everything society demanded of us. We got married, we raised a family, paid our bills, and gave of our time and energy to the community. What more can we do? Evidently our best efforts and intentions are not enough to get us to the end of our exploring.

So the next stage comes when, angry and bitter perhaps, we become determined to go it alone with no help from anywhere. We finally learn that life is a lonely road. We shall just have to make the best of it out of the rubble and debris of our broken hopes and shattered aspirations. It is in this loneliest, driest part of the desert, that the second metamorphosis occurs. The camel changes into a lion, and this king of beasts is determined to be master of all, even if he is only sovereign of a desert place. There he will yield no allegiance to any god save that of his own will. Yet even this is not enough. After the strivings of the lion cease, the spirit is transfigured into a child. The lion's role is to say "No" to the universe. Only the child in us can turn that bitter "No" into a liberating "Yes." Becoming a little child again after being a rampant and angry lion is hard. Only a childlike acceptance of those broken pieces, those shattered fragments we call our life, points a way out of the wasteland, out of the desert, out of the dark wood.

The childlike "Yes" is essentially a movement of love, a cry of wonder, an act of worship. This theme of worship, as an obedient "Yes!" of surrender, has been beautifully explored by Peter Shaffer in his play *Equus*. The plot is concerned with a psychiatrist's struggle to "cure" a seventeen-year-old stable boy who has gouged out the eyes of six horses. The play may not reflect sound psychiatric theory and practice but it does raise fundamental and searching questions. Shaffer's point is that human beings, to be human, must have an object of worship, a form of allegiance. Mystery is at the heart of human existence, and it is a mystery which ultimately claims our obedience, demands our "Yes!" The psychiatrist is brought face to face with this mystery, with his own mystery, when he confronts the stable boy in his particular pain and horror. Through a peculiar set of psychological circumstances the boy has made the horse the object of his worship; one night as he tries to make love to a girl in the stable (surrounded by six horses in their stalls) he realizes that this is an act of betrayal. He is being unfaithful to his god, to the god who is even then watching him commit apostasy. In a wild fury the boy attacks the horses and gouges out their all-seeing eyes.

The psychiatrist is faced with an obedience gone wrong, with a "Yes" given over to an inadequate sign of the mystery. Yet he is fascinated by the boy. He envies the young man's passion and wonders if the only cure is to rob him of his object of worship. To rob a person of his object of worship would be to perform a lobotomy of the soul.

The doctor worships nothing. He is a contemplative but only by way of being a voyeur. If he has a passion at all it is classical Greece, but then only through the middle-class medium of glossy pictures in coffee table books. He longs to recapture the wonder of childhood. The child is a natural contemplative. The child can teach the adult how to say "Yes" again. "Look!" exclaims the psychiatrist, Dr. Dysart, "Life is only comprehensible through a thousand local gods. And not just ten old dead ones with names like Zeus, but living geniuses of place and person! And not just Greece but modern England! Spirits of certain trees, certain curves of brick wall, certain chip shops, if you like, slate roofs—just as of certain frowns in people and slouches . . . I'd say to them— 'Worship as many as you can see—and more will appear!' "[17]

The "Yes" of the child is an ever-expanding one to all that the world offers. The more we take time to be still, to contemplate, to see, the more the gods appear, the more the mystery unfolds itself. The image of God is seen more clearly in our brothers and sisters, in the gods of self-forwardness which give our life meaning and purpose.

The psychiatrist's dilemma is that he can see these gods but something holds him back from passionate worship. What he sees does not conform to what "normal" people call normal. Worship, adoration, is that which fools us out of our limits; it breaks open what we think of as normal. Normal is a double-headed god. It can mean the smile in a child's eyes, but it "is also the dead stare in a million adults. It both sustains and kills—like a god. It is the ordinary made the beautiful: it is also the average made lethal."[18]

The journey does come full circle and invites us to become a child, to wage war on the destructively normal. This is not a journey back into childishness nor into the senility of second childhood. Rather it is the journey home to stand as naked as the day we were born before the mystery of being. The psychiatrist is made naked and vulnerable by the pain he meets in the boy. He realizes that he can no more comprehend the reality of a horse then he can the mind of a child. The horse, *Equus,* stares at the doctor: "Do you really imagine you can account for Me? Totally, infallibly, inevitably account for Me?. . . . Poor Doctor Dysart."[19]

To cure the boy, to make him normal, the psychiatrist has to take away his passion, his obedience, his object of worship. The boy worships the horse; idolatrous and even demonic, at least he worships, at least he has said "Yes!" to something. Every three weeks at midnight the boy would strip off his clothes and gallop naked into the night on the back of his sweating and steaming god and would ride until he collapsed with exhaustion.

Dr. Dysart is unnerved. He hesitates to take away the boy's pain and tries to explain his hesitation to his friend. His dilemma is this. Pain is a peculiar human possession; not the pain arbitrarily inflicted on us by others, but the pain which inevitably comes to us on our pilgrimage. That kind of pain is unique to the individual. To take away the boy's pain would be to take away his passion. This boy had felt intensely. He had at least galloped!

To go on this journey and to call it yours you first have to get your own pain. It is the pain of being born again out of the labyrinth of your wanderings. It is the pain of seeing the glory of things in all their blinding radiance, even if only for a moment. Yet while my pain is peculiar to me, it is also a *shared* pain. The journey through pain to glory is always in the company of others as we attempt to utter the great "Yes." We must slip our hand into the hands of those on either side of us. What we could not do alone, perhaps we can do together. The wounded image can be restored, but it can only be healed and made beautiful as we travel together hand in hand. God has been with us from the beginning, our secret and often hidden companion.

12.

The Journey and the Journey's End

CONTINUAL PILGRIMAGE

> Then I saw a new heaven and a new earth, for the first
> heaven and the first earth had vanished, and there was no
> longer any sea. I saw the holy city, new Jerusalem, coming
> down out of heaven from God, made ready like a bride
> adorned for her husband. I heard a loud voice proclaiming
> from the throne: "Now at last God has his dwelling among
> men! He will dwell among them and they shall be his people,
> and God himself will be with them. He will wipe every tear
> from their eyes; there shall be an end to death, and to
> mourning and crying and pain; for the old order has passed
> away."
>
> Then he who sat on the throne said, "Behold! I am making
> all things new! . . . I am the Alpha and the Omega, the
> beginning and the end."
>
> *Revelation 21:1–6*

We have traveled a long way on our journey. We must travel
the road out of the wasteland as a little child. We have to grasp
the hands of the ones we find on either side of us. Our lion-heart
with its reliance on reason is no doubt excellent within its own
sphere, but our reason is not sufficient when confronted with all
that is, when faced with mystery, when we have entered into our
own mystery. We need to walk with others, to see what others have

seen. We cannot do it alone. Our common journey is to heaven. We journey because we feel something of eternity in our veins. We are not quite at home here.

The English poet Edmund Spenser, in about 1580, wrote these words in *The Faerie Queene:*

> And is there care in heaven? and is there love?
> In heavenly spirits to these creatures base,
> That may compassion of their evils move?
> There is: else much more wretches were the case
> Of men, than beasts. . . .

How does the Christian traveler know that there is care in heaven? Is there really this transcendent image stamped on the human heart? Even the most cynical would admit that we hunger for something above and beyond us which we might (stretching things a bit) call heaven. But what heaven is or what it is like we have no idea. The Christian Gospel claims that we *can* have a hint and foretaste of that which we call heaven now. Jesus Christ in his death, resurrection, and ascension has made the great journey already.

One of the great visionaries and voyagers of the last century was the poet William Blake. When he looked at the sun, he did not see merely a round disk of fire. He saw an innumerable company of the heavenly host, crying, "Holy, Holy, Holy." Blake, as unorthodox as he may be, really did *see* the mighty sun in a way not open to dull souls.

What insight, then, does Blake throw on the Christian pilgrimage? For him we are only fragments of Christ. We are scattered, splintered, separated from life by our willfulness, and Christ and his angels are abroad looking for us to bring us home. Christ is the mighty hunter of our scattered fragments. He seeks us everywhere even in the "land of unlikeness" where the image has been forgotten. He is there in our darkness calling us home. Hence our long, painful yet wonderful adventures.

The journey, then, is a return, it is a going home. It is the pilgrimage of the prodigal, and the entry into our kingdom is through the saving death of Christ. How so? It is the secret of the dying life for the sake of love. Christians have a lover who is willing to go to the ultimate length for the sake of love. This is the mystery of the death of God: not as understood by the necessary, if pessimistic, theologies of the 1960s but as the expression of a wild kind of loving we can scarcely comprehend. The Christian heaven is presided over by the broken and wounded God; a scandal to those who will not dare to enter into their own mystery.

When will we begin to see? When will we begin to contemplate? The Greek word for contemplation is *theoria,* and it was used to describe that state when man is fully awake to all that is. To contemplate, then, is to wake up! To be fully present to all that *is* involves a drastic kind of self-emptying (Nirvana again), not to remain empty but to wait in the stillness for the recreative word of God.

There comes a point in our lives when we have to stop running. Constant activity that is not undergirded by a genuine inner peace is worse than useless, because activity unfocused and undirected is a fearful form of slavery. We get caught in the dreadful pattern of the cause and effect of our own actions. There are moments, however, when we have an opportunity not to act but simply to be. It is those moments we must treasure.

As I sit in my study looking out the window at the beautiful trees, it dawns upon me with full force that I have little idea of what a tree is. One of them is particularly striking. It is majestic. Hardly discernible among the leaves is an enormous split between the two biggest branches. In the gap are the signs of rot. That tree, like all trees, is marked for death. Herman Hesse, one of the contemplatives of this century, writes of an old peach tree in his garden which had been uprooted by a storm. It was as if the fabric of reality itself had been torn, and through the gaping hole there appeared the terrors of the abyss, meaninglessness, futility, and terror. Not even trees are to be trusted. They too disappear eventually into the great darkness.

To journey home is to step into the great darkness and wait.

"Darkness and Light, to thee are both alike, and the night is as clear as the day" (Ps 139:12). When we begin to see, the dazzling light of reality appears to us as a deep darkness. So Plato, in the seventh book of his *Republic,* compares mankind to prisoners in a dark and gloomy cave. And St. John of the Cross, when discussing the dark night of the soul, writes: "The self is in the dark because it is blinded by a light greater than it can bear." I am "blinded" even now by the reality of the tree which stands outside my window, just as Dr. Dysart in the play *Equus* was "blinded" by the reality of the horse. How much more am I blinded by the dazzling darkness of God himself.

The essence of the tree escapes my reasoning. How bankrupt I feel when I try to look into my own mystery. The Christian claims that the clue to our human mystery is found in the life, death, and resurrection of Christ. St. Paul, in Colossians 1:27, puts it this way: "The secret is this: Christ in you, the hope of glory to come." In the Christian vocabulary, glory simply means being-in-all-its-fullness: that in itself is the beginning of a definition of heaven, a hint as to the nature of the treasure we seek on this pilgrimage. Contemplation is the word we use to describe the means by which we see, by which we catch a glimpse of joy. Christ has begun in us the restoration of the image, the imprint of God.

That hope of glory to come is the one imprint on the human psyche that transcends all the other imprints and, in the end, saves us from them, saves us from the downward pull of each of them. The trauma of birth, the power of the mother, the feeling of defilement, the mystery of sexual identity, and the molding influence of family and society—all are transcended and transfigured by the hope of glory, which is the imprint of God, the Blessed Trinity.

This is the Christian mystery, proclaimed as Good News. The imprints do not have a permanent hold on us. We discover that there is such a thing as human freedom, however fragile and limited it may be. It is the freedom to embrace hope. This is Gospel. We do not have to remain trapped in our psychologically determined prison.

As we have seen, the Christian doctrine which attempts to put this into words is that of the creation of mankind in God's image. We are, individually and collectively, made in the image of the invisible God. What does that mean? How do we resemble God? How do we have a share in divinity? We are like God insofar as we are free. The journey home is the pilgrimage to liberty. It is the freedom to fall, to die, and to be born again.

The doctrine that we are made in the image of God means that we have the terrible gift of freedom. It means that we are not merely members of a species gifted with intelligence. To be an *imago Dei* is to be a person—unique, particular. The image is defaced insofar as we are reduced to a number, to a function, to a stereotype. To be "imaged" means that there has never been anyone exactly like you, nor will there ever be again. It means you can say "I." To be a human being, to be made in the image of the Blessed Trinity involves having a story to tell. "Man was created," proclaimed St. Augustine, "in order that a beginning might be made." We pilgrims have barely begun, for we are only what God is planning, and he is always calling us to a fuller and freer life.

The doctrine that we are all descended from Adam boldly affirms that, insofar as a human being allows the image of God within to have free rein, he or she *is* Adam, is an incarnation, a manifestation of all mankind. In this sense we are called into being as persons, not by a mere biological process, nor by a determinative psychological one. We are called into being by God in such a way that our being depends on the existence of others. We are who we are, not by biological fiat, but by our interaction with others, with our enemies as well as our friends. As mere biological specimens, we would be incapable of sin. It is as free persons that we become guilty or glorious or both.

Becoming a person means, in Christian terms, the restoration of the image of God within us by the grace of the Holy Spirit. Grace, the power of God, is the means by which the imprints are traversed. That transfiguring imprint of the *imago Dei* was with us from our beginning. We carried within us that aching and mysterious emptiness. No one has the last word about any of us because of that desert place within, and even our self-judgment is liberatingly penultimate.

How is this hope, this restoration of the divine image, born and nurtured in the human heart? If we are designed to be in communion with God, if God is our lover, then we have to indulge in the things that lovers do. The lover wishes always to be in the loved one's presence, and to gaze and to hold. The name for this loving regard is contemplation. Again and again on our journey we have been confronted with this indispensable and supremely human activity called contemplation. It is an act of love, a gazing at and an entering into reality. It is not something only for adepts or experts. This loving gaze is open to everyone. For the Christian, it means seeing the patterns in life through the prism of the Bible, and through that crucial encounter with Christ in the broken bread. There, for us to see, to touch, and to eat, is that power-bearing bread which speaks of brokenness and healing, of death and resurrection.

As we begin to *see* daily we begin also to live within a mystery, not a blind fog but an incomprehensible certainty. Reason is *not* discarded, and science is put in its correct place; that is, it is afforded a place of honor and commands our respect, but its wider pretensions with regard to mystery and meaning are displaced. Contemplation, seeing, becomes an integral, vital concomitant of journeying, of pilgrimage. It requires a peculiar concentration and discipline as the way gets more and more wonderful and unfamiliar.

If we are to journey home and become what we are, sharers in divinity, we must really begin to see and hear in earnest. As George Eliot said, we must "hear the grass grow, the beat of the squirrel's heart, the roar on the other side of silence." Our own odyssey is a seeing and a hearing that takes practice and involves pain. The pain is there because, as we have been told often enough, mankind cannot bear very much reality. The discipline on the journey is not for its own sake, but rather to increase our capacity for bearing reality, for bearing glory, for learning to bear being-in-all-its-fullness. That is why we must try to see what others have seen. We must walk with a Blake, with a Homer, and with a Dante. We must live within the vision of glory given in Scripture and Eucharist.

Dante's *Divine Comedy,* culminating in the *Paradiso,* is the journal of a pilgrimage to heaven. Homer's *Odyssey* is a tale of a return, a journey home. Both Dante and Homer knew from within themselves the wanderings of the human spirit.

Dante did not remain in the Dark Wood. He saw through the darkness a mountain illumined by the sun's rays and knew that it was to that bright mountain he must journey. His guide, the Latin poet Virgil, explained to the inexperienced pilgrim that there was no way he could make the ascent directly. He must first descend into the infernal regions, to the bottom of hell itself. Only then could he climb the mount of Purgatory. Virgil, who symbolized unaided human reason, could take Dante only to the gate of heaven. Another guide was needed. It was Beatrice, who represented divine wisdom. She, and she alone, could lead the pilgrim into heaven. It is strange that the journey home involves a route away from the familiar and the commonplace.

There is a case history reported by Dr. Robert Gerard of Los Angeles[20] of such a descent and return by one of his patients. It illustrates the perennial power of the ancient symbols and the vital part they play in human development. The patient in question found himself in the depths of the ocean struggling with an octopus which threatened to engulf him. He was asked to see himself rising to the surface of the waters accompanied by the menacing octopus. At that moment, the monster transformed itself into the likeness of his mother. So far, this case history follows a now rather hackneyed pattern. The mother figure rises to the surface as possessive and devouring. But there is an important sequel. The patient was told to climb a mountain and take his mother with him. As they mounted higher and higher, the patient began to see her differently. She began to lose her menacing power, and, for the first time, he was able to see her as a human being in her own right. On the top of the mountain mother no longer threatened her son, and he was freed to love her as a human being. Here the menacing imprint of mother is overcome, not by her destruction but by transfiguration. Only after the ascent can the son see that the mother has been the victim of his fears.

The upward pilgrimage into these heavenly places where we are transfigured into persons is a difficult one. It threatens with destruction. Both mother and son had to make the ascent and jettison the security and comfort of established roles and comforting projections.

We have seen, in the varied richness of world literature, abundant documentation of this ascent, this journey home. It might be good now to see the journey through the eyes of one of the great religions. Let us make the journey home through the steps provided by the mythology of Islam.

In Islamic mythology, the soul has to journey through seven heavens. Dante himself was influenced by the Islamic form of the pilgrimage, and the *Divine Comedy* is based, in part, on Moslem sources. Mohammed, according to legend, paid a nocturnal visit to purgatory, hell, and heaven. Each stop on the way is marked by a star and each star has its own angel-guardian.

The first heaven is made of silver and is the realm of Adam and Eve. This is the world of the "fall," the theater of mankind. This is only the first step. Adam's journey has hardly begun. As we have already seen, there are many dangers ahead. In fact, as Goethe says, "the dangers of life are infinite and safety is among them." The human journey through the world of the fall, through the kingdom of anxiety, is a call to face alarming possibilities. T. S. Eliot's depressing vision of the future is turning out to be true. He saw a colossal planned boredom; classless, faithless, frontierless, rootless; deprived of poetry, of historical consciousness, of imagination, and even of emotion.

The uprootedness of Adam's realm leads to a great deal of pain and distress, for we exacerbate the problem by beating one another over the head with our own unhappiness. We scramble into "religion" and talk ourselves out of meaning. "Poor talkative Christian-ity," says E. M. Forster. Adam talks too much and laughs hardly at all. Only the child knows how to laugh freely, because the child is totally present, totally *at home* in his world. The Zen Buddhist tradition bears witness to the fact that one of the best ways to meditate is to stand with your hands on your hips and laugh uproariously for ten minutes. Laughter is a great antidote to the petrifying influence of our anxieties and can, if embraced as a child, lead us out of the realm of Adam.

The second heaven is made of gold and is the realm of Jesus and his herald, John the Baptist. It is the arena of history. The rump, that poor remnant of the old Israel, of all that is human, resides in Jesus, and we are to rediscover our humanity in him. We have seen that we discover our identity by identifying with someone or something. What does it mean to identify with Jesus? For those early Christians, it meant facing the charge of atheism. We must never forget this. Here was a new and thoroughly alien way of looking at the universe. The refusal to offer a pinch of incense to the emperor was not only politically subversive, but also atheistic with regard to the basic, accepted belief of the divinity of the universe. It was atheistic in the sense that it questioned the exis-tence of the whole established order and refused to make obeisance. Christianity is as radical as that.

Jesus was a scandal; peculiar, particular, one of a kind. He was seen as the beginning of a new species. To the Christian he is no mere avatar, one incarnation among many within the historical process. He is a new beginning. It is this particularity, this scandal, this historicity, which enrages many students of mythology and religion. The late Alan Watts, for example, could embrace death and resurrection as an idea but not as an event. Yet Christianity seen as Gospel, gift, grace, stakes its life on the priority of the God who manifests himself in and through the events of history. It is neither a philosophy nor an ideology, but a proclamation of what *happened.* What happened is summed up in the affirmation: "Jesus is Lord." Because he happened, nothing was ever quite the same again. In the light of this new reality focused in Jesus, how am I to behave? What ought I to do? Religion has to answer this basic question. Buddhism answers it by dispensing with moralism and by denying the very existence of the ego. "What ought I to do?" is a nonquestion. If there is no self, there is no one to take free responsibility, and without freedom or responsibility there is no point in talking in moral terms. But without freedom and responsibility there is no humanity either. This form of surgery is too drastic. For what is a human being if he is neither free nor responsible?

The danger of our uncritical attraction to the religions of the East and to popularized psychology is that we easily mistake their ideas for reality. The ideas beget a system by which we can ascend to heaven. We end up with a "sacred way" which we can all see but never follow. This makes everyone a Sisyphus, rolling his rock almost to the top of the mountain, but destined to slip back again and again and again. Jesus, like the Buddha, becomes yet another in a long line of Christ figures, moral teachers who can effect nothing.

A Buddhist once said that the real difference between Christianity and Buddhism was that Jesus was the son of a carpenter, whereas Buddha was the son of a king. This expresses a genuine difference. The earthiness of the origins of Christianity is very important and we would do well to be at least as critical of other religions as we are of our own. There is a great deal of sentimentality attached to the Western view of Eastern religion. It is not easy for the Western mind, however well-informed, to appreciate how deep the idea of impersonality goes in the thinking of the East. We have tended to romanticize it and ignore its more questionable manifestations: the caste system, indifference to hunger and disease, and a strange compassion that fails to enter into the world's sufferings. The compassionate Buddha, in contemplation, radiates love for the whole universe. He is not proficient at translating that radiating love into action. Joseph Campbell, who is hardly a supporter of the Christian view of things, insists that we must abandon

the image "of a sort of pre-Raphaelite Buddha-soul sitting harm-
lessly on a lotus, deliquescing into nirvana with love for all beings
in his lotus heart." Buddha, as well as Jesus, has to be demytholo-
gized. Infuse the Eastern view with an unashamed occidental spirit,
and that attractive enigma, that mighty "ego-less ego," such as an
Alan Watts, is the result.

Christianity, like Judaism, stands or falls on its belief that history is the theater of God's activity. Time is a creature like the rest
of us, and, while all things are swallowed up by it, it is the arena
of our soul-making, or, if you prefer, of our becoming persons.
Time is part of our journey through life to its end, which is death.
The second realm through which we must pass is history, time,
where we come face to face with Jesus as an historical person. The
second step is necessary; without it, Christianity degenerates into
an attractive but pathetic idealism.

The third heaven, of pearl; and the fourth, of white gold, are
presided over by the angel of death and the angel of tears. Pearl
is the realm of Azrael, the angel of death. He is forever writing in
a large book the names of the newly born, and blotting out the
names of the dead, as they leave their earthly existence. We have,
at this point, to face judgment and recognize and acknowledge all
that we are, all that we have ever done. After death we see things
clearly for the first time and cannot but weep at our betrayals, at
our Judas acts, at those looks from people we have harmfully
touched. They remind us of the way Jesus must have turned and
looked on Peter after his triple denial. There, in the fourth heaven,
shedding ceaseless tears for the sins of men, is the angel of tears
whose height is five hundred days journey.

We shed tears for the failure of the Church, yet even there we
find hope. Tears are cleansing. We weep, too, for the world. Our
all too secular world has lost much of its seductive power. It has
become such a mess that we yearn to rediscover a Christianity
with substance and power. Until recently, it was assumed by
many that the Church had everything to learn from the world,
and very little to teach. Now things look somewhat different. An

English friend of mine wrote to me recently commenting on his visit to New York:

> I think New York is conducive to the discovery . . . that Christianity has daring, searching and demanding things to say to the actuality of men—not flat men but three-dimensional, shadowed by death.

Tears, too, are necessary. The Church, to my mind, has become far too jolly and cheerful. Continuous resurrection is a right reaction to the sterile God-is-dead theology, but it is very exhausting carried to excess. Unless there is a genuine dying of self, there is less and less of a self to be resurrected.

And beneath the tears there is also danger. There are, in Northern Ireland, Protestant women bravely and unobtrusively crossing the Shankill Road to pray with the Catholics on the other side. There are still places on this planet where to pray is to risk your life.

There are other reasons to weep. We shed tears because the book of life has apparently fallen into the hands of men and women; because politicians as well as others claim to *know* the will and mind of God, the express intentions of Jehovah. I am fearful of those who know the mind of God, who know what I am and what I want, behaviorally and politically. I am fearful of my own priesthood and I am fearful of the two priests within me; of the one who bleats traditional formulae drained of all their ancient power (as if nothing had happened in the realm of thought over the past fifty years); of the other who mouths the new vocabulary with such ease. This priest within is the clerical equivalent of the Watergate brigade. That burning truth hits me again and again. I am what my brothers and sisters are. I stand or fall with them. If I am to be human at all, if I am to get off the ground and fly, I must do it with others. I feel something like that fabulous Chinese bird, the *chien,* which has only one wing and one eye. Two of these birds must unite in order to fly. The one-eyed and one-winged partner who joins with me in flight may not always be the one I would have chosen. But I cannot fly alone.

There are tears (the angel, remember, is five hundred days journey high) because too few of us, one-eyed and one-winged as we are, have been willing to accept the reality of the partner, of the vocation given us, and soar into the air. We have consistently failed to draw the life out of the Christian story and unlock its mystery. Our religion tends to render us little or no experience, but only authorized, worn out clichés. Efficient and renewed as we are, there is no fire in the belly. We are like the blacksmith in the Hasidic tradition who wanted to go it alone. So he bought a hammer, an anvil, and bellows. But nothing happened. There was no flame, no heat in his forge. It seems to me that we have everything except "the one thing needful"—the spark, the fire. We have smart, efficient bellows, shiny new anvils and enormous hammers, but as yet, no fire.

The fifth heaven, of silver, is presided over by the avenging angel. Our infidelities, stupidities, small-mindednesses turn out to be very expensive. They must be paid for, atoned, Without forgiveness we cannot proceed. We need to recapture the notion of sin, not in its awful, narrowly moralistic sense, but as a description of that state in which we find ourselves as human beings, the state from which we need rescue.

We need rescuing from ourselves, from our self-image, from the narrow world of our conscious experience. Having rightly embraced a deep experimental Christianity, we need liberating from the idol of seeing our present experience as total. All of us are prone to embrace a spiritual parochialism. We are, as Christians, to breathe the air of the new age, of the age that is coming. Solzhenitsyn's *Lenten Letter* reprimanding the Patriarch of Moscow for giving in to the culture is interesting in this regard. He accuses the Russian Church of failing to affirm the truth that the human spirit, fortified by the grace of God, is stronger than the current social milieu or cultural climate. One could argue that the Russian Church can be excused the compromises. We, in the West, have not been harried by the state. Yet we have, without political pressure, embraced the values of this present age.

A sense of sin is very bracing and fortifying in regard to our culture, because it does not allow us to accept the *status quo* or assume the normality of this present time. Personally and socially, a proper sense of sin keeps us on the move. It demands that we try to see life as all of a piece, that life does hang together with a desperate seriousness so that every little thing we do makes a difference to the color and shape of the universe. The avenging angel is everywhere guarding the integrity of things.

No doubt, you may say, one can go too far. Where is the laughter, which you claim to be so important, in the midst of all this seriousness? It is precisely this: that if we do take the interconnectedness of things really seriously, we are saved from moralism and hurtled into the realm of pure grace. To see things this way leaves no room for Pelagianism (that is, saving ourselves by pulling up our own bootstraps, or embarking on a course of moral self-improvement). In the face of all these interconnections, only two things are possible: despair, or a Gospel of healing and forgiveness. This is what Camus saw when he asserted that the only serious question is that of suicide. There are many, many ways to kill yourself without the outer world even noticing that you have done so. The roads to self-slaughter are many.

If Camus is right, what alternative is there to suicide? "The canon 'gainst self-slaughter" runs deep within us. Something has to die, but suicide is not the way. Suicides used to threaten the collective peace of society. They were denied burial in consecrated ground because theirs was the fearful, despairing affirmation of meaninglessness, of ultimate bankruptcy. Times, fortunately, have changed with regard to our attitude toward suicides. There is a growing recognition today of a right to die with dignity as well as a right to live. Christian dying is a very different matter. It affirms within the very act of dying the promise of resurrection, of new life. It means dying to one life, rising again to another, and living from a new center, which is God. This is what St. Paul meant by his "dying daily." We long to yield, to abandon ourselves to something. To yield to anything less than God is, in the end, a form of suicide.

We cling with a wild perversity to the belief that we can save ourselves by acts of self-justification, by a new asceticism of good works done to a needy and grateful world. The more confused and lost we are, the better it must be, since we shall have become identified with the world and its lostness. We have a strange and perverse equation: Gospel = freedom: freedom = being as confused and lost as possible. Our spirituality, such as it is, glories in this perversity. Ours is like the Indian discipline of reversed seasons. We do everything backwards. In that discipline, the ascetic, as the year becomes warmer, puts on more clothes; as it grows colder, he takes more off. So we, when we are confused, add to our confusion. We rarely allow our activities to be fed by balanced contemplation.

Death! Tears! Vengeance! These are the three realms of judgment. But they, too, must be put behind us. They have to give way to the sixth heaven, which is made of ruby and garnet. It is the realm of heaven and earth, and is presided over by that prophet of prophets, Moses. The angel who guards it is made half of snow and half of fire.

As we have progressed, words have become more and more opaque. How do we speak of the ineffable, the word beyond words? All we can do now is to look and to listen: "Do you not hear the deeper song?" Why do we not see the healing and the remedy that is right under our nose, right in our own heart? Hell and heaven are very close. They exist cheek by jowl.

In Sartre's *No Exit* all the characters could have been the agents of each other's salvation. We are shown an empty room in hell. A man is ushered in, followed later by a woman, and finally, in comes another woman. That is all. They are there forever. The reality of hell resides in the awful fact that not one of them can change. The man needs the sympathy and understanding which only the older woman could have supplied. She, in turn, is fiercely lesbian, despises the man, and looks to the younger woman for love and companionship. The latter, on the other hand, has eyes only for the man whom she could not possibly understand or help. Later on in the play the door of the room opens and they are free to leave. But they prefer hell. No one dares step out into the unknown. We seem to prefer our petty hells rather than face the possibility of new beginnings. All of us, one way or another, are at root fiercely conservative. Even the "with it" and the "trendy" among us cling tenaciously to yesterday's modernity and are unable to see its imprisoning datedness. We are perpetually out of date. Just as the world is turning to religion, when there is a guru under every tree (or stone), the Church is modeling itself, parodying itself, on IBM.

The person who is only out-of-date by a decade is less willing to change than the hardened traditionalist. The former assumes he is already modern and up-to-date, so what is there to change. We do not have the imagination it takes to think of heaven, to contemplate new and wonderful possibilities. We are trapped by our selves. Once we accept rescue from the self-trap, there are no limits to what is in store for each one of us. Christianity may yet take us by surprise as we discover it is true. Heaven is the enemy of the average and mediocre within us and, if we wish to remain just as we are, we would do well to repudiate the possibility of an abundant life beyond our wildest dreams.

There is the story of the atheist in *The Brothers Karamazov*, who, after death, was sentenced to walk a billion miles as penance. He lay down in the road and refused to walk for a million years. He eventually dragged himself to his feet and unwillingly walked the billion miles. When he was finally admitted to heaven, he declared that it would have been worth walking ten times as far for a mere five minutes of heaven. Such is the seventh heaven, which is divine light itself. It is praise and adoration, integrity—all. It is beyond the power of tongue to describe. In Islamic mythology it is ruled over by Abraham. Each inhabitant is bigger than the whole earth and has 70,000 heads, each head has 70,000 faces, each face 70,000 mouths, each mouth 70,000 tongues, and each tongue speaks 70,000 languages, all chanting the praises of the Most High!

The journey ends in adoration, praise, and thanksgiving. "Journeys end in lovers meeting." We share in a painful glory, in a bloodstained victory, in a sacrificial triumph. It is the life of joy and penitence, of suffering and happiness, of glory and pain. It is this fundamental act of adoration that unites who and what we are into an organic whole, that puts the dismembered fragments of our selves back together again.

So we have come through the desert, the wasteland, the dark wood, and yet they are ever with us. We are always journeying, yet our lover is always with us. The seven heavens, the myths and legends of the heroes of mankind, all bear witness to the journey. It takes on different forms. Some scarcely know there is a journey, some stumble blindly along the way, others are given something of the vision by which human beings are given the grace to transcend themselves and are transfigured into persons.

What of the Christian pilgrimage, that adventure anchored in history, in now, and yet seen stretching throughout eternity? The way the Christian approaches the great mystery, the way he attempts to understand the world, the way he tries to integrate his experience and make the journey inwards, is through the power of sacrificial love as a pattern of death and resurrection. It is a universal pattern, found in all religions and in all places. The theme of the miracle of life by means of death echoes throughout the human drama. The Christian does not, however, claim that he has "arrived" while the rest of humanity stumbles blindly in the dark. He lives continually within a mystery, and for him that mystery is not light, insight, illumination, so much as "the deep but dazzling darkness." St. Augustine in his treatise on the Trinity writes this concerning man's search for truth: "We have found, not the thing itself, but where it is to be sought: and that will suffice to give us a point from which a fresh start may be undertaken."

Our life is a series of "fresh starts," of never arriving, yet always within the presence of that mystery which drives us on. That mystery is personal, that mystery is a person, that mystery is

Christ, and Christ's strange work among us is precisely the restoration of the lost image, the reforging of the sixth imprint. The fact that we are always having to begin again and again need not cause despair because we are moving, in Him, from glory to glory, from what is less real to what is more real.

The key to the Christian story is the resurrection, which will, in the words of St. Gregory of Nyssa, "bring about the restoration of our human nature in its original form." That is, a human nature free and loving. The resurrection of Christ was the supreme Christian event after which nothing was the same. Thus the distinctive and awe-ful part of the Christian drama is its concrete, fleshly quality. Christianity claims that the idea and the reality are one in Christ. It happened once and for all and, because it happened, everything else changed. By the grace of God, then, the Christian exchanges the fatalism of religion, of the cycle of birth and death, for the terrifying freedom of the kingdom of God whose call is *not* predictable, where the *new* is always breaking in. We exchange the tranquillity of Nirvana for the blustering power of the spirit and find within the very center of the whirlwind "the peace of God which passeth all understanding" (Phil 4:7): a costly peace forged by Christ on the cross. In Austin Farrer's phrase, we are to exchange "our living death for his dying life."

The knowledge of death, *our* death, is a great gift. Death is our companion, always there by our left shoulder reminding us of who and what we are. It is the gift of selfhood. Christianity is not a way of safety. We can only live freely with that which we are willing to lose. Christianity is a way of love. It is a journey with love and into love that risks everything. It is continual pilgrimage.

As we have seen, time and time again there is no easy way. Sybil, the attractive voyager in Charles Williams' novel *The Greater Trumps* had to make the terrible journey before she could begin to see. She was the calming spiritual power in a family full of conflict. The forces of good and evil raged throughout the story in cosmic fury. It was her quiet strength of mind which lent itself to the forces of good which, after a bitter struggle, triumphed in the end.

The freedom to yield, the freedom to be spent in the service of others is hard to come by. It means making the pilgrimage from Bethlehem to Calvary, from Christ's birth to his death, from our birth to our death. This is the supreme *peregrinatio,* the greater inner journey of those who follow in the steps of all who have known an exodus of some kind. The Children of Israel had to leave Egypt, to "die" in the desert. Indeed, this was the accusation the Hebrews hurled at Moses: "Have you brought us into this desert to die?" Moses, who had encountered the living God in the burning bush, answered, "Yes!" He knew that the rabble he had led out of Egypt could be forged into the People of God only by means of "death and resurrection."

Christians are the people of the Exodus and know from their master that their freedom is supremely manifest when they are prepared to lay down their life. Their freedom is the freedom to die. We now come to the heart of darkness which is the blinding light of new life; the mystery of the cross. Let us enter the mystery of the death and resurrection of Christ, the heart of the Christian story.

In the drama of Christ's death and resurrection we may hear the word beyond words, the deeper song that echoes through the universe and within every human being. We may discover the "great thing" which calls us. There are many rhythms, many variations in counterpoint. Another writer would use different words to sing the same song, but the tune that I now sing, I trust, may find echoes in your own.

13.

The New Path

A DEEP BUT DAZZLING DARKNESS

Early on the Sunday morning, while it was still dark, Mary
of Magdala came to the tomb. She saw that the stone had
been moved away from the entrance, and ran to Simon Peter
and the other disciple, the one whom Jesus loved. "They
have taken the Lord out of his tomb," she cried, "and we do
not know where they have laid him."

John 20:1,2

By baptism we were buried with him, and lay dead, in order
that, as Christ was raised from the dead in the splendour of
the Father, so also we might set our feet upon the new path
of life.

Romans 6:4

Here St. Paul describes the whole purpose and glory of the
resurrection of Christ: that "we might set our feet upon the new
path of life." The old path led to one place only, to the gate of
death. But in Christ, death is done to death, death is swallowed up
in victory. Christ opens up a radically new path, a new way of being
human, yet still we find it hard to believe because, as Kierkegaard
knew, it is hard to obey.

Is this new path really possible? There is no doubt that we long
for one. We are forever undertaking new journeys, new quests of
the spirit, in the hope that there may yet break forth a path which
would bypass every obstacle, including death, our old enemy. We

may dabble in *I Ching* or *Hare Krishna,* try the tarot cards or the Ouija Board; anything to relieve our boredom and lostness. Some of us may even be tempted to try a minicourse in Christianity.

We find it hard to see the journey as all God's work; it is God's gift. He is the journey itself as well as its end. We are like Sisyphus rolling a great stone up a hill and forever slipping back, little realizing that the only stone between us and salvation has already been rolled away: the stone before the tomb of Christ. The one stone, the stone of death, which we could not remove ourselves, has been moved.

The destiny promised is beyond the grave and adds a dimension to the present life which is indescribably joyful. We are on a new path to a new humanity. Life is always far more than we actually *know* of life, but in the first spring of our love, we imagine that we can make the dead world live. We stubbornly persist in thinking that we can accomplish this, that we can make it on our own, that our love will conquer the world.

In myth and in legend the magic stone was sought by many. This philosopher's stone would raise gold out of lead, would raise men from the dead, would turn suffering into glory. Always we are searching for a resurrection, sadly ignorant of the one that is being offered us in Christ. The stone which men and women sought in vain was also a tomb. The pilgrimage in its own way is always a way of death. The only stone promised here and now is the one engraved *Hic jacet,* here lies. And so our life is cluttered up with a host of "if onlys." If only I had done this or that instead of ... Our life becomes a list of what might have been and we become creatures with a past but no future.

Nothing we could do, or can do, can change this. We, our lovers, our children, are marked for death. This is not morbidity. This is brute fact. We finally come up against confusion, futility, and the deadliness of death in the face of which we can do nothing. But perhaps God can! Perhaps he and he alone can set our feet on the new path of life. This is the Good News: that in the face of our helplessness God has acted.

Picture for a moment the gate of death. My study in England

was dominated by an enormous Victorian engraving of this solemn subject. It hung over the fireplace, a sermon in black and white for all who entered. It was given to me by an anonymous donor. Here was a picture of the angel of death standing by a doorway. He (she or it?) was kindly helping all who came through the gate into the next world. The picture was particularly striking as nearly everyone was in a frantic state of undress. There was a cardinal, a drunk, a soldier, and a whore, all waiting to pass naked into judgment. One figure had obviously been called to meet his maker during the course of a cricket match. There he stood, head bowed, still dressed in his white flannels, cap, and blazer, clutching a cricket bat under his arm. It was a very English picture! There the Christian and the English myths had become thoroughly mixed up together. How we laughed at the scene and ridiculed the sentimental and syrupy vision of our forefathers! But after a while, that strange and silly picture got to me. My laughter became a little uneasy, more subdued. The picture of me going naked into the arms of death did not seem all that funny after a while. Death is no laughing matter, yet, in the face of it, this is about all we can do.

The picture, in the end, did me a great service. It did what every Good Friday should do. It placed me and my whole life exactly on the threshold of death. We see ourselves placed in the light of the last severity, the last hope. We see the dead and realize that what passes for our life is a living death. That is exactly what we are: dead. We hope for the risen life and realize that is exactly what we are not: risen. The power of the resurrection is the coming together of what we are and what we are not. We are to surrender what we blindly imagine we are in order to become the glorious wonder that we are destined to be. The greatest strength of our life is the power to lay it down. It is nothing, a dead thing, while we hug it tightly in our arms. Instead of trusting in the ancient and blooming tree of life, we plant shrubs of our own and keep digging them up to see if they are alive.

We find as we tread the new path of resurrection that two things begin to happen. We begin to *mean* something, and we realize that we all belong to one another. There is one journey, one story, one destiny. The individual is drawn into the fellowship of the Church, and the Church is the fellowship of the resurrection. We gather round a common table where bread is broken and wine is poured. At this table we are given two gifts, or rather, a double gift of crucifixion and resurrection, for the two always exist together. In the words of St. Gregory Nazianzen: "We are to bear everything that Christ bore—the nails, the death, *and* the resurrection." Are we ready to bear the glory of God, to bear the resurrection?

Here is not a solution but the illumination of a mystery. The resurrection illuminates for us the inwardness of things and brings us a knowledge of our buried life. Life is seen for what it really is: inexhaustibly concrete and everlastingly strange. We see things differently. Something new is happening to us, a new path of life; what the early Christians simply called *the way*. From the inside we begin to see what it means to do or refuse an act of courage, to grieve over sins, to be transfigured by love. Faced with this direct confrontation with reality, we know that God does not die when we cease to believe in him. We do. But we die creatively when we believe in him.

Death is a fact, a brute fact. So is the resurrection, which makes the brutality of death endurable. The Christian as the supreme realist is committed to live according to the facts. "God so loved the world" (Jn 3:16). It is a fact. In a world where there is evil and pain, this assertion is no cheap trick to fool us into a drugged euphoria. The crucified Christ reveals the unfathomable cost of that love.

Nothing, then, can destroy us. Everything that kills the human heart has been done to death on the cross. The fifteenth-century poet William Dunbar expressed the Christian struggle in this way:

> Done is the battle with the dragon black
> Our champion Christ, confounded this his force
> The gates of Hell are broken with a crack
> The sign triumphal raised is of the Cross

> The devils tremble with hideous voice
> The Souls redeemed to bliss can go
> Christ with his blood our ransom does endorse
> *Surrexit Dominus de sepulchro.*

And Henry Vaughan two centuries later:

> Death and darkness get you packing
> Nothing now to man is lacking
> All your triumphs now are ended
> And what Adam marred is mended.

We know the wild change that comes over someone who has fallen in love. We know the transfiguring power of someone who knows, really knows, that he is loved. There is a wildness which can be very alarming. We should not be afraid of being a little wild, and considered rather odd, for we know that we are loved and that is cause enough to make us light-headed. It is intoxicating and, if we really took God at his word, could transform this cold death-dealing world. After all, there were only eleven at the beginning, and they were not terribly distinguished. But they surrendered to the love of God and exploded all over the world!

How else do you account for the wild explosive power of the saints? St. Francis, says Brother David, S.S.F., had a head-on collision with this rock, his risen Lord. It knocked him silly, but it knocked him and many he touched into the kingdom of God. Perhaps it is time for us to have a head-on collision with the risen Christ, be knocked off course and into a new path of life, to do this even at the risk of looking somewhat foolish in the eyes of the world.

It was Lady Julian of Norwich who beautifully affirmed the ultimate optimism of the Christian: "All shall be well, and all shall be well and all manner of thing shall be well." We find that, in spite of all the disillusionment and pain at the breakup of our ideals, the Christian story ends on a note of triumph.

At the conclusion of Malory's *Morte D'Arthur,* Sir Lancelot and his companions have all retired from the world in order to live as hermits. Among their company is a retired Archbishop of Canterbury. One night every one in the little monastic community is disturbed by the sound of the archbishop's loud laughter. The companions gather round his bed and wake him up, and the archbishop cries, "Ah, Jesu mercy, why did you wake me? I was never so merry, and so well at ease in my life." They asked him why. He had seen Sir Lancelot's soul being received into heaven by myriads of angels, and he laughed and laughed and laughed.

The Christian quest ends with the sound of laughter in heaven. "There," says St. Augustine, "we shall rest and we shall see, we shall see and we shall love, we shall love and we shall praise." All this can begin in us now even in the middle of our pilgrimage.

May we be given the courage to let the good things in us run wild and so be changed from glory to glory. This is our destiny, the end of all our journeying: to live within the deep but dazzling darkness of the love of God.

> *To see thee is the end and the beginning*
> *Thou carriest me and thou goest before*
> *Thou art the journey and the journey's end.*

Notes

1. George Orwell, *The Collected Essays, Journals & Letters Vol. II* (New York: Harcourt, Brace & World, 1968), p. 15.
2. Joseph Campbell, *The Masks of God* (4 Volumes) (New York: The Viking Press, 1970).
3. In *Myths to Live By* (New York: Bantam Books, 1973), p. 207ff.
4. Ibid., p. 216.
5. St. Augustine, *Confessions* (Book X); see the Penguin Classic Edition, R. S. Pine-Coffin, trans., 1961. p. 212.
6. Quoted in *The Paradise Within,* Louis L. Martz (New Haven: Yale University Press, 1964), p. 18.
7. *The Poems of George Herbert* (London: Oxford), p. 156.
8. Ibid., p. 176.
9. Ursula Le Guin, *The Farthest Shore* (London: Puttin Books, 1971), pp. 197-98.
10. Monica Furlong, *The End of Our Exploring* (London: Hodder & Stoughton, 1973), p. 53.
11. Rosemary Haughton, *Tales from Eternity* (New York: Seabury, 1973), p. 73.
12. John Donne, *Collected Sermons* (Vol. V) ed. Potter & Simpson (Berkeley: University of California Press, 1953-1962), p. 38.
13. *The Complete Works of Alfred Tennyson* (New York: R. Worthington, 1877), p. 230.
14. Ursula Le Guin, *A Wizard of Earthsea* (London: Puttin Books, 1973), p. 56.
15. George Orwell, *The Collected Essays, Journals & Letters Vol. IV* (New York: Harcourt, Brace & World, 1968), p. 137.
16. Campbell, op. cit., Vol. I, p. 125.
17. *Equus: Shrivings* (New York: Atheneum, 1974), p. 61.

18. Ibid., p. 63.
19. Ibid., p. 74.
20. Quoted by Roberto Assagioli, *Psychosynthesis* (New York: Viking Press, 1965), pp. 212–13.

Bibliography

No one writes in a vacuum. This book is the result of my thoughts forcing themselves to be written down. It would be impossible for me to acknowledge adequately my debt to all those who have stimulated my thinking over the last decade. The immediate stimulus for this work was my reading of Joseph Campbell's four-volume work, *The Masks of God,* but the main thrust of the book itself is the result of my conducting quiet days, retreats, and seminars on the spiritual journey and the life of prayer.

What follows, then, is a partial bibliography of those recent works which have set me thinking.

Assagioli, R.: *Psychosynthesis,* Viking Press, pb., 1971.
Brooke, P.: *The Empty Space,* Pelican, pb., 1972.
Campbell, J.: *The Masks of God* (4 volumes), Viking Press, 1973.
———: *Hero with a Thousand Faces,* Viking Press, 1973.
———: *Myths to Live By,* Viking Press, pb., 1972.
Cocteau, J.: *The Difficulty of Being,* Coward McCann, 1967.
Cox, H.: *Seduction of the Spirit,* Simon & Schuster, pb., 1974.
Dunne, J.: *Way of All the Earth,* Macmillan, pb., 1972.
Eliot, T. S.: *The Complete Poems and Plays,* Harcourt, Brace & World, 1967.
Fremantle, A., ed.: *The Protestant Mystics,* Little, Brown & Co., 1964.
Furlong, M.: *The End of Our Exploring,* Hodder & Stoughton, 1973.
———: *Contemplating Now,* Westminster, 1972.
Hesse, H.: *My Belief,* Farrar, Straus & Giroux, 1975.
Houghton, R.: *Tales from Eternity,* Seabury Press, 1973.
———: *The Theology of Experience,* Newman, 1972.

Jung, C.: *Memories, Dreams & Reflections,* Collins & Routledge & Kegan Paul, 1963.

———: *Modern Man in Search of a Soul,* Harcourt Brace Jovanovich, 1955.

Kazantzakis, N.: *The Saving of God,* Simon & Schuster, 1960.

Keen, S. & Anne Valley Fox: *Telling Your Story,* Doubleday, 1973.

Kirk, R.: *Eliot and His Age,* Random House, 1972.

Kopp, S.: *Guru,* Science & Behavior Books, 1971.

———: *If You Meet the Buddha on the Road, Kill Him!,* Science & Behavior Books, 1972.

Laing, R. D.: *The Divided Self,* Pantheon, 1969.

Malraux, A.: *Antimemoirs,* Harcourt, Brace & World, 1968.

Martz, L. L.: *The Paradise Within,* Yale University Press, 1964.

Merton, T.: *Asian Journal,* New Directions, 1973.

———: *Contemplative Prayer,* Image, pb., 1971.

Murdoch, I.: *The Black Prince,* Chatto & Windus, London, 1973.

Roszak, T.: *The Making of the Counter-Culture,* Doubleday, pb., 1969.

Saurat, D.: *Gods of the People,* John Westhouse, 1947.

Steiner, George: *In Bluebeard's Castle,* Yale U. Press, pb., 1974.

Watts, A.: *In My Own Way,* Pantheon, 1972.

Wiesel, E.: *Souls on Fire,* Vintage Books, pb., 1972.

Williams, C.: *Arthurian Torso* (ed. C. S. Lewis), Oxford University Press, 1948.

———: *The Greater Trumps,* Avon, pb., 1969.

Zachner, R. C.: *Drugs, Mysticism and Make Believe,* Collins, 1972.